BORN A BEACHCOMBER

BORN A BEACHCOMBER

Thomas Mathieson

as told to
Steve Mathieson

The Shetland Times
Lerwick
2014

Born a Beachcomber.

First published 2014.

© Steve Mathieson.

A catalogue record for this book is available from the British Library.

ISBN 978-1-904746-89-8

Printed and published by
The Shetland Times Ltd.,
Gremista, Lerwick,
Shetland ZE1 0PX.

To Hilda

BORN A BEACHCOMBER

Chapter One

A fine snow powdered the land around Burrafirth on the day I arrived in the world, 15th March, 1918. This was a mere few months before the end of the Great War, although the trials and troubles of those involved in that deadly conflict obviously meant nothing to me at the time. However, many of the families of the crofters and fishermen struggling to scratch out an existence on our windswept islands in the North Sea were feeling the desperate emptiness that accompanies the loss of sons, husbands and fathers in the grinding cogs of war. The next world war would have another deep impact on the men and women of Shetland generally, and also myself personally, but that was over twenty years in the future, a lifetime for some in those days.

As the youngest of eight children I was never short of company and one or other of my siblings would usually be somewhere near at hand to keep an eye on their boisterous little brother. Antonia Margaret (born 1900) was the eldest, being nearly eighteen years old by the time I was born. The next in line and eldest boy was Alexander who was born in 1902, followed by James Andrew (1904), William Gilbert (1906), John Charles (1910), Ann Tamar (1912), Jemima Grace (1916) and finally myself. I was followed by in 1919 by a younger sister, Agnes, but unfortunately she died at six months, becoming yet another statistic of the high infant mortality rate still prevalent in the islands at this time.

Life on a small Shetland croft in the early part of the twentieth century was a tough existence and a constant struggle for survival, with little or no paid work available in the islands for my father, Jimmy Andrew. Both my mother and eldest sister, Antonia, had worked as "gutter lasses" during the boom years of the herring industry in Baltasound, when the seasonal population of Unst would soar to over 10,000. They had gutted and packed

Father, Jimmy Andrew Mathieson, 1941.

Ann Tamar, aged 16, 1928.   *Antonia, aged 18, 1919.*

herring into barrels at fishing stations specially built to cope with the hundreds of small herring boats that would offload their catch each day, but by the 1920s demand had peaked and Baltasound was seen as too distant from the markets to be economically viable, the industry now vanishing as quickly as it had first appeared.

Keeping a croft in those days was a subsistence lifestyle, relying on what we could grow, catch or barter, and though this kept us poor we always had food on the table, even in the leanest of times. We kept six or seven cattle and a dozen hens on the croft around the house, and forty ewes with lambs on the hill scattald on Hermaness, the hill that formed the western side of the entrance to Burrafirth and in which we held a share, while the rich waters would provide a good return for an evening's fishing. Burrafirth itself was gouged out between two towering hills during the last ice age and our house lay on the eastern side of the voe in the southern lee of Saxavord where the fine soil provided good crops of tatties, neeps and cabbage.

Our mother, Dorothy, who was forty-three years old when she gave birth to me (my father was forty-five), would make an early start to the day's chores and be busy downstairs by five o'clock, turning the old ashes over and putting on new peats to get the range cooker fired-up and reinvigorate the kitchen with heat and life. Antonia was next up and would make her way out into the chill morning air with an empty pail and a wooden stool to see to the milking, while Ann would manoeuvre the old cast iron frying pan, the size of a dustbin lid, onto the hob. Mima's first task was to climb the cold, dank staircase to the boys' room, to shake us out of warm, comfortable dreams to face the shivering reality of a damp bedroom often made arctic by the wind that whistled in around ill-fitting sash windows.

As soon as I was awake I would pop out of the bed I shared with Willie and Johnny and hurry over to the window, rubbing eye-holes in the condensation and peering through to the outside world, particularly in the direction of the beach. In spring and summer the first sounds that greeted you in the morning were the cries of the kittiwakes that lined the cliffs and rocks of the bay, though their numbers have declined dramatically in recent years. The best mornings were those when the sun reflected off a calm sea, lying beneath the banks like a framed mirror in the bay below, and my thoughts turned to wandering the long, golden sands of Burrafirth and an early morning search for the kind of treasure that wind and tides might have washed ashore in the night, or perhaps exposed in the shifting sand. Alex had left for the lighthouse service by the mid-1920s leaving the three younger boys to talk excitedly about getting down to the beach whenever we had the chance, though we knew that we had our duties around the croft to perform first.

As the youngest my first job in the morning would involve scampering down the stairs and out the kitchen door to the hen-house, usually still in night-shirt and bare feet, to gather the morning's eggs from beneath the reluctant, scolding hens. I would then hurry to deliver them to Mother, stood ready at the stove, with a large dollop of fat now sizzling away in the over-sized frying pan. If we were lucky there would be bacon to accompany them, and at the right time of year we would also have wild mushrooms which were abundant in the surrounding meadows.

As the smell of the breakfast cooking mingled with the usual background smells of the peat burning in the range and the fish drying on the overhead runner alongside the newly-washed clothes, the aroma would permeate the upper floor of the little house and inspire father and my brothers to begin the trek down to the kitchen. By the time they arrived, yawning and pulling up their braces, mugs of scalding tea were being placed on the table by my sisters. The pail of frothy, warm milk had been placed in the corner of the room by Antonia on her return, and into this was now dunked a blue china jug, which was then placed in the centre of the table. The jug then did the round of each at the table in turn, a splash of milk for each teacup, with the youngest son forced by an insistent mother to drink a mug-full while it was still warm from the body-heat of the cow. Pasteurisation was not a process that we concerned ourselves about at that time.

As breakfast came to a close Father, Jimmy, Willie and Johnny would get up from the table in their own time, put on jackets, boots and flat caps, and with a brief nod of appreciation to Mother disappear one by one out into the fresh morning to begin their tasks for the day. By 1925 all my brothers had finished school and could concentrate on the jobs that needed doing around the croft. In fact by now they were taking over from Father, who was spending more and more of his time in Aberdeen, where he worked on the quayside as a fish "splitter", a job for only the hardiest of men, as it meant working at all times of day and night and in all weathers, splitting open the fish that arrived in port packed in ice, using a specialist set of knives that he proudly kept razor-sharp. The money he earned at this work paid for all the provisions, implements and little luxuries that we needed to buy, and though it started out as seasonal and occasional work, after a few years he began to spend the majority of his time in Aberdeen with only the odd trip home.

By the time the men were leaving, Mother and my three sisters would be well into the rest of the morning chores about the house, which meant I was pretty much given a free rein to do as I pleased, as long as I didn't get under anyone's feet. Once Mother had scrubbed my face and neck and dressed me in various items of my brothers' out-grown and cast-off clothing I'd be ready to explore my options for the day's entertainment. The weather would determine whether my adventures would take place inside or out, either option being fine by me as our cottage and barns seemed big as a castle and full of dark nooks and crannies that contained any number of mysterious, forgotten objects. Of course I preferred to be outside if possible, with endless opportunities for exploration and less chance of being discovered and stopped by one of the grown-ups. If, for any reason, Mother forbade me from going to the beach, I would often head for the well at the back of the house, as from there I could decide to follow the burn either upstream or down, where it's course formed a small valley that fell towards the sea and was the perfect place for setting up a secret camp. Innumerable ancient dykes criss-crossed the land out beyond the course of the burn, all now grassed over, and become raised walkways to follow into the wilderness towards Saxavord. The well was, of course, the only source of fresh water for the house, as it would still be many years before plumbed water appeared in this part of the world.

Our home was called Buddabrake, a warm name that matched the genial atmosphere to be found within its walls. It was a typical storey-and-a-half crofter's cottage of the time; whitewashed stone walls built six feet thick in places to withstand the incredible gales that regularly lashed our exposed islands and to retain the heat generated within, with a porched entrance leading into a narrow hallway, stairs leading to two bedrooms on the first floor, and on the ground floor a but and ben. Lack of space due to having a gaggle of children had led my parents to give one bedroom at the top of the stairs to the boys and the other to the girls. Their bedroom was the ben-end, so my father had knocked an internal door through from the but-end into the single-storey barn attached to that end of the house, and this he had converted into our kitchen (and wash-room when required).

This room was the real heart of the house, containing an old china Belfast sink, a peat-burning range for cooking and for heat, above which was a wooden runner on a pulley from which hung everything from clothes and blankets to mutton, fish and even seaweed. There was also the dining table and chairs, other assorted easy chairs including two rockers for my

Lower and Upper Buddabrake, 1930s. (Courtesy of Shetland Musuem and Archives)

parents, a spinning wheel, an old black, iron, foot-pedal sewing machine, and the old tin bath for when a proper clean could be avoided no longer. Electricity, like plumbed water, was a luxury that had not yet reached the homes of most folk in Shetland, so oil lamps served to provide the only light during the long, dark winter months, their flickering luminescence casting unsteady shadows through the low-ceilinged interior and giving a semblance of strangely-distorted life to everyday objects.

There was still an exterior door to the back of the kitchen, which, as it was sheltered by the hill into which the house was partially built, in winter months served more as a main door than the west-facing porch entrance to the house. The small internal door at the far end of the kitchen led through to what had now become the first barn, which was full of all manner of fishing and farming paraphernalia, was where the dogs slept, and also housed the plank and bucket arrangement which was our toilet. From here another connecting door led to the byer, which would house the cattle through the worst of the winter, and would normally have a sheep or two tied up prior to slaughter. If anyone walked through the byer and barns to the kitchen without closing the doors behind them then the smell that arrived with them would be a pungent aroma of animals and excrement that could literally bring a tear to the eye.

If the weather was good there was only one place to head for on most days, and that was to the golden sands of Burrafirth beach. Once you reached the cliff-face, perhaps a hundred yards from the house, there was a steep, zigzagging path to be negotiated before you finally reached the sand. Though we used this path from an early age and knew it like the back of our hands, it was not without its perils, and once caught out my brother Willie, who was in his late teens at the time. We were heading for a night's fishing on this particular occasion, marching single file in the deepening twilight. The Wellington boots we wore were not designed to provide good grip on a steep, grassy, cliff-face path at the best of times, and on this occasion Willie was carrying a box of fishing line and never noticed that the previous night's rain had washed a small section of the track away.

In front of me Willie disappeared straight over the edge, tumbling into the darkness with a brief shout of surprise. We heard his grunted exclamations as he hit the sand-stone cliff-face whilst falling, then finally the sound of his body thudding onto the sand below. All was silent then, and we feared the worst as we hurried down the remainder of the path to where he had fallen. As we approached the spot where he lay we were pleased to hear some hearty curses through the half-light, which meant that at least he was still alive, and to our relief found him sitting up waiting for us. He had fallen fifty feet at least, but it appeared that it had all happened so quickly that he had remained relaxed and simply bounced off the rocks on the way down. His face was covered in blood from superficial head wounds, but he hadn't broken a single bone and had had the presence of mind to protect his head as best he could during the fall. He had definitely had a lucky escape, though he didn't come out entirely unscathed. As a consequence, perhaps, of the shock of the experience, in the following days and weeks he lost all the hair on his head, which was never to grow back fully again.

Once you had negotiated the pathway down, the first thing you came across at the bottom, next to a little burn that gushed and chattered down through the rocks and twisted across the sand to the sea, were the fishing boats. These were Shetland Models, clinker-built, traditional boats, light enough to be hauled across the sand by two men and for those two men to row out of sight of land, but strong and seaworthy enough to sit steady on a North Sea swell while you were fishing and get you safely back to shore if you got caught out by a sudden squall, as would often happen in these latitudes.

Two of the boats were in good working order, ready to go to sea, but there was a third, Spider, which had seen the end of her useful days, and was now pulled up onto a natural platform in the wall of the small ravine cut by the flow of the burn. Her paint was flaking, and small mosses and clovers were beginning to sprout through her planks, but she still served a purpose as a perfect playground for the children of fishermen. Many journeys were undertaken, sea battles fought and acts of piracy committed, without Spider ever getting foam on her prow.

Once we had tired of causing imaginary mayhem amongst the world's merchant fleets we would turn our attention to the beach itself. I say "we" because I had plenty of playmates in those days. Often it would be my cousins Willie and Bertie Mathieson from Lower Buddabrake, our nearest neighbours, or one or two of the children from the crofts nearby. Burrafirth was a thriving community in those days, as was Petester, a little collection of houses on the side of the Loch of Cliff, about a mile up the hill from the beach. Our family of ten was by no means considered unduly large then, and both Burrafirth and Petester had enough children to each fill their own schools. The beginning of the end for those happy times came with the building of the first proper road through the island, which was to leave Burrafirth isolated as one of its northern outposts, and meant extinction for Petester as a community, because the road never reached it.

View of Buddabrake from Burrafirth beach, 1938.
(Courtesy of Shetland Musuem and Archives)

Burrafirth beach was a magnet for the local children, a dynamic, ever-changing playground containing all the elements necessary to excite the imagination of a young mind. On a spring tide at low water the sand was endless, and we would range far out searching for "spoots", or razorfish, in shells about six inches long. They would poke up out of the sand about half the length of their body, delighting us by spitting out a spout of water before retreating back under the sand, and if we were quick we would catch them before they disappeared.

These low tides would bring my father and older brothers out too, carrying narrow-headed Shetland spades with a single footrest on one side. They weren't interested in spoots, they were looking for "giddeks", or sand-eels, which we would use to bait the lines prior to a night's fishing. In those days the sand was alive with them, though in these days of over-fishing they've become a much rarer commodity, not only for fishermen but also for the great variety of seabirds, including puffins and guillemots that depend on them for their existence.

There were plenty of rock pools to explore as we ventured further along the beach, usually concealing a crab, shrimp or small fish or two to keep us interested. Then there was the chance of finding some flotsam that had washed up on the previous tide, most of which, especially if it were timber, would be utilised in some way on the croft: very little went to waste in those days. In fact, as we grew older, we came to realise that what we found on our beachcombing trips was an integral and important component of life on our islands. Because of Shetland's lack of trees and our lack of currency to buy timber from the south, most of the wood we used for fence-posts and furniture came from the sea. Although we learned this trade on Burrafirth as children it wasn't long before we were familiar with most of the shoreline of Unst and knew the best spots to search when the wind was blowing in any particular direction. The west coast would draw bounty in directly from the Atlantic currents, Woodwick being particularly well named, and a heavy sea washing a deck cargo off a passing ship would end up as a god-send for needy islanders.

Burrafirth would have otter tracks to follow, seals basking on the sand and the rocks which would always, to our frustration, notice us long before we could sneak up on them. There were stranded starfish and jellyfish to be poked at, crabs scuttling amongst the seaweed, migrating trout and eels in the burn and, above all, the constant cacophony of the seabirds. As previously mentioned the cliff walls were white with nesting kittiwakes throughout the spring and summer months, and the noise these small, delicate gulls could generate was truly stunning. Mallies (fulmars), the birds who would later usurp the nesting sites around the bay, were fewer then, as were the predatory bonxies (great skuas) and black-backed gulls that would patrol the nesting colony, looking to pick off the unwary or unguarded. Gannets, puffins, guillemots and razorbills could all be seen fishing further out across the water, while shags and cormorants would sit on the rocks sunning themselves.

The West burn meandered out of the Loch of Cliff through meadowlands splashed with the vibrant colours of dog violets and marsh marigolds, across the sand flats and down the west side of the beach to the sea. Once we had waded across, turning stones with our toes to flush out eels, we had a choice of direction if we were to continue our explorations. Head south around the west shore of the loch and we would come to Petester, but continue around the far shoreline of the firth and head north and we would firstly reach the "fort", the remains of a ruined broch sat in front of our cousin's house at Stackhoull, from where we had a clear view north to the mouth of the firth and the great cliffs of Saxavord. Stackhoull was known locally to have been where the Viking chieftains of old had lived and maybe hidden their treasure, so was always a popular spot to find children poking sticks into rabbit-holes and straining to turn rocks over, anxious to see a glint of gold.

We would often sit and imagine the thoughts that perhaps went through the minds of the Pictish fort-builders when the first dragon-prowed longship was sighted, cutting through the waves and entering the sheltered waters of the firth. Would the women and children have stayed within the protective confines of their stone-built round-house while the men gathered on the beach, ready to fight the invaders and defend their land and families, or would they have gathered up what possessions and livestock they could and hurried off to hide in the hills? As children we always imagined the glorious battles our Viking ancestors would have fought to claim possession of this land, but in reality the original Pictish inhabitants probably wouldn't have stood much chance of prevailing against the battle-hungry sea-warriors who were making their mark on the world at that time.

Further on from the fort stood the Ness, an oblong-shaped, two-storey building containing separate quarters for the families of four lighthouse keepers. With its elevated position on a natural promontory of rock and its looming stone walls topped with crenulations it looked for all the world like a real castle to us youngsters. The keepers served the Muckle Flugga lighthouse, Britain's most northerly inhabited point, the lighthouse having been designed by the father of Robert Louis Stephenson, and built in 1824. Robert Louis himself had visited whilst the lighthouse was under construction, and the legend is that he based his map of Treasure Island on the outline of Unst. There is definitely a distinct similarity to be seen, though I believe that at least one other Scottish isle claims to have provided similar inspiration. My family had a link with the lighthouse since it had first begun illuminating the wicked crags of the Flugga, as we provided the majority of the relief boat crew, ferrying keepers and supplies to the rock when required, quite often in appalling conditions. This tradition would continue from the 1820s through to my brothers Jimmy, Willie and Johnny (Alex became a keeper himself, though not in Shetland) until automation meant the end of a manned lighthouse service at the Flugga in the 1980s.

We always enjoyed visiting the Ness shore station, as one or other of the keepers would invite us in for a bite to eat, and as their wife was preparing the food they would entertain us with stories of haunted lighthouses, of huge serpents from the depths that had been attracted by their light, and of course tales of ships who ignored their warning and wrecked themselves on the jagged rocks, their occupants casting themselves out into the raging seas, from which few ever gained the sanctuary of dry land. An hour or two of cakes and tall tales would fortify us for the trek home, and keep our young minds busy as we delighted in re-telling each other all the gorier parts of the stories we'd heard, though my older sisters would not be so impressed. My sister Ann was often a companion on my beach adventures, and, although she was six years my senior, joined in with my games enthusiastically. She had a lively imagination and was adept at turning the objects we found on the shore-line into toys and treasures, and was a firm favourite with all the younger children. She never had a chance to entertain children of her own, alas, as her life was cut short in 1934 when she died of septicaemia, at the age of just twenty-two.

The freedom I had enjoyed thus far in my life came to an abrupt and unwelcome end in autumn 1924, when I was sent to school. In truth I didn't have far to travel, just to the local school in Burrafirth itself, a twenty minute walk across the heather. In a way I was lucky to be educated in the 1920s, as there were over eighty schools in Shetland at that time, including twenty so-called "side schools". These were sited in some of the more far-flung communities, including Burrafirth and Petester, staffed usually by a willing though less than fully-qualified teacher to service those children unable to travel easily to one of the larger schools. It felt like the end of the world to me, and for the first few days my mother would have to drag me there, until I found that the academic life did have its compensations.

That compensation was in the form of one of my new class-mates, Cathy Scott, the daughter of one of the lighthouse keepers at the Flugga. There were never more than ten children in the whole school at any one time, but despite this, and despite my tender years, I had found my first love. Cathy I found far more interesting to study whilst in class than my form work, a view unfortunately not shared by my teacher, who also happened to be my aunt Osla. The first time I was caught paying more attention to my sweetheart than to my study was the first time I felt the sting of aunt Osla's knitting needles across my knuckles, but not, I'm afraid, the last. Cathy was the prettiest thing I had ever seen, with corn flour gold tresses, eyes as blue as a summer sky, and the memory of her is still as fresh as if we had sat together in class only yesterday, instead of being separated by nearly ninety years.

We were at ease with each other immediately, in the way that only children can be, and thereafter would spend every spare moment in each other's company, whether sitting in the field at playtime making daisy chains, turning stones over in the burn to catch eels, or running out of school at the end of the day with aunt Osla hot on our heels. This friendship carried on happily for a year, but then, as with all things in life, had to come to an end. News came through that her father had been posted to another

Burrafirth school, c.1925. From left – back: Phyllis Caird, Mima Mathieson, Nellie Scott, Tina Mathieson. Middle: Willie Stickle, Daisy Caird, Billy Foster, Bill Sinclair. Front: Bertie Mathieson and Tammy Mathieson. (Courtesy of Unst Heritage Centre)

lighthouse, and so, after a child's fleeting goodbye that happily lacks any realisation of its true and permanent meaning, Cathy had to leave. Of course, I never saw her again.

After four happy years at the Burrafirth School it was time to move on to the secondary school at Haroldswick. If I sometimes had cause to be upset with what I felt was harsh treatment from aunty Osla, I was to find that this was as nothing compared with the regime I was about to encounter. Haroldswick School was approximately three miles from home, which equated to a pleasant thirty-five minute amble on a summer's day, or an hour long, full-blown polar expedition when winter had set in. When the weather was at its worst, of course, mother had no choice but to keep

Burrafirth school with Auntie Osla, c.1928. From left: Bertie Mathieson, Ian Hughson, Willie Mathieson, Osla Betty Sutherland, Billy Foster, Tammy Mathieson, unknown, Ronnie Foster. (Courtesy of Unst Heritage Centre)

us at home. Perhaps "choice" is the wrong word, as sometimes when there had been a heavy snowfall the weight of the snow would prevent doors and windows being opened, and much as mother might want us out from under her feet she found herself thwarted by the conditions.

Inclement weather, however, did not evince any sympathy from the headmaster as an excuse for being late. Time would have to be made up after school, but only after "six of the best", as a sound thrashing with the cane was known as back then. Of the three teachers at the school, who were all well respected for their teaching ability, two were easy-going and even-tempered, but the headmaster, Mr Taylor, was a man who was not easily pleased, though we tried hard to stay in his good books. He was a World War One veteran, and we heard had suffered in the Flanders trenches all the horrors that the first "modern" war had introduced. It was common knowledge that he had been wounded in action, surviving the conflagration but emerging in a condition known as "shell-shock". He was probably a very brave man who had been through appalling experiences, but I do not believe this left him with the ideal temperament to run a school.

Shortly before I joined he had been reported to the School Board for thrashing one of the girl pupils so hard that her arm was badly bruised and swollen, so much so that in fact they had feared it broken. He was reprimanded for this, but it was not considered a reason for removing him from the school. An edict was passed preventing any further corporal punishment for girls, a decision that seemed to so enrage him that, unfortunately for me and my fellows, he decided to counter it by redoubling his efforts with the boys.

Though I was the recipient of beatings on a reasonably regular basis, on one infamous occasion I was fortunate enough to be a non-participatory witness. You could normally tell from first thing in the morning if this was to be a bad day for one of his black moods, as he would sit silent as the pupils entered the class, scowling darkly and watching for the first indiscretion from an unwitting victim. The class would sit nervously and quietly, realising that this was no time for thoughtless chatter that may single you out for special and very unwelcome attention. On this particular Friday, although there was tension and an air of foreboding about the class, we managed to reach lunchtime with no-one having irritated Mr Taylor unduly. Immediately after lunch, he called my cousin, Bertie Mathieson, and me over to his desk, and we feared the worst "Tom, I want you and Bertie to take a bucket each and go collect the potatoes, and make sure you get enough to last us the week."

Like many schools at that time, Haroldswick had its own vegetable patch, and on a summer's day nobody minded missing an afternoon's education for a chance to get some fresh air out of sight of authority. Bertie and I sighed with relief, "Yes sir."

With no further encouragement we were gone. We started with the best of intentions, and made a good start to our labours, intending to work at the tatties for an hour or two, and keep the head happy. Not long after we'd begun filling the bucket, however, we heard a commotion coming from the classroom we'd recently vacated. The window was around the corner from the vegetable patch, so Bertie and I stood up from the line of potatoes we were working on, abandoned our bucket, and quietly crept around the side of the building.

We carefully raised our heads and peered in the corner of the window. Having recognised the early sounds of the head working himself up into one of his rages, we were not surprised to see him towering over the desks of two of our classmates, berating them for some unknown misdemeanour. The pair of them sat cowering, looking up at him wide-eyed in the knowledge that they were likely to be on the receiving end of a thrashing in the next couple of minutes. Unfortunately one of the miscreants had the temerity to argue his innocence; I don't think Mr Taylor could believe his own ears, but certainly the effect upon him was spectacular. Instead of fetching his cane, this time he leant down and picked up the desk, which was one of the old fashioned oak types that had the seat (and child) attached. This he then thrust into the air above his head, the occupant hanging on for dear life. The whole lot was then swung around in the air, much in the manner of a hammer-thrower beginning his rotations, with books, pens paper, and ink flying out of the desk at all angles, accompanied by the terrified screams of the victim.

After several turns the desk was sent back to earth with a thud, Mr Taylor's face had faded from purple to pink, and a shocked silence settled on the class as the miscreant loosened his grip on either side of the desktop and settled as deep into his seat as possible. As Mr Taylor caught his breath to further berate the unfortunate youth Bertie and I looked at each other and slunk back to our potatoes, glad that we had had been sent out before we could possibly have been involved in the scene we had witnessed. Before we knew it the four o'clock bell sounded and we realised we had only barely filled one bucket all afternoon, knowing that the head would not be pleased with our exertions. We trudged unhappily back into school with our miserly contribution to the week's meals, and bumped straight into Mr Taylor who was marching out to find us. We expected the worst and braced ourselves for the blast, but he simply looked down at us in a strange, almost sad manner, and carried on past without a word. As often happened, the storm of his rage had abated, and so for the second time that day Bertie and I were on the receiving end of good fortune rather than a beating.

Having described Mr Taylor as I have, it would be remiss of me not to mention the other side of his character. He was undoubtedly a very fine teacher even though he now lacked his pre-war temperament, was very astute academically, and was a great boon to the brighter children of the school. My cousin, Robert Mathieson, was an exceptionally talented student, and Mr Taylor helped him secure a university place at a time when very few Shetland children went on to higher education. The head also surprised me when it was my time to leave, at the age of fourteen.

"Will you stay on another year, Thomas, and see how things work out? I believe you have the potential to achieve your qualifications."

"I'm sorry, Mr Taylor, I've already accepted an offer from a shipping company down south to start as an apprentice engineer, so you see it's impossible for me to stay at school" I lied, as by now I was determined to leave but lacked the courage to simply give him an outright refusal. I did, in fact, intend to go to sea when I left school, but as the youngest my mother was keen on keeping me close at hand, and it was to be another six years before I was able to follow my own path. In the meantime there was work to be done at home, and, unwilling though I was to pull my weight with the more unpleasant chores, there was always plenty found for me to be getting on with.

BORN A BEACHCOMBER

Chapter Two

Though we were poor in financial terms our diet was as good or better than the majority of folk enjoyed in Scotland at that time, and would probably even be considered healthy in these modern days. We grew our own potatoes, cabbage, turnips, carrots and lettuce, had fresh milk and eggs to hand, and when we ate meat it would be our own lamb, chicken and occasionally beef. One of the biggest parts of our diet, however, was the bounty from the sea. My father would be out in the boat laying lines most evenings, sometimes remaining out fishing all night. As we boys grew older we would join him on his trips, and would normally return with a good haul of haddock, cod, ling, saith, tusk, flounder, halibut, herring, mackerel or trout. When I was young I would only be allowed to undertake fishing trips to the "eela" (near the coast), staying within sight of the shore, but later on I would undertake the trips to the "haaf", the deeper fishing grounds, twenty miles and more from land, which was a hard haul for a twenty-feet long boat propelled only by a scrap of sail and a good set of oars.

On one such trip we were approaching the fishing grounds, Jimmy and Willy pulling on the oars while father prepared the lines at the back of the boat, myself in the prow as lookout. The sea had a decent swell on, though the weather was clear, when I noticed a commotion in the water ahead of us, where it seemed to me that something large was moving around on the top of the water. This sent a shiver down my spine, just in case it was one of the fabulous but dangerous sea creatures the lighthouse keepers had warned me about. It turned out, as we neared the creature, that it was indeed a monster – a monstrous-sized skate. It was splashing around for all it was worth, and seemed to be attempting to swim back down under the water, but something was obviously preventing it. It didn't take long to catch the unfortunate fish, but a while longer to land it on the boat, as we estimated it to weigh well over a hundred pounds. Once on board my father investigated further into what had caused the skate to remain on the surface, and determined that it had a massively enlarged liver, which had stopped it re-submerging once it was up.

There was now no room for anyone to actually fish from the boat, let alone room for anything else we might catch, so we headed back to shore. Once there I was sent scampering off to fetch a friend of ours who owned a horse and cart, while the rest of the crew struggled to carry the skate up the cliff path. The monster fish was then transported to the Baltasound Hotel, approximately four miles away, where the proprietor, with all due solemnity, handed out a dram of whisky to each of the three of them and agreed to pay £8 for the prize, which was a small fortune then.

Exciting as we thought our fishing expeditions were, they couldn't compare with some of the harrowing tales we heard occasionally concerning our grandfather, Scollay. Gaining his unusual Christian name from his mother's maiden surname (she was Barbara Scollay), he had been a fisherman of the old school, skippering a sixareen, a thirty-foot descendent of the old Viking longboats, which was powered by a square sail or six oars. These boats were widely used in Shetland from the early eighteenth century right up to the late nineteenth century, and at the height of their popularity over five hundred boats were operating crewed by more than three thousand Shetlanders. Scollay could be said to be mostly Viking himself with piercing blue eyes, six-feet tall and solidly built, strong of arm and a will of iron, and as at home on the open ocean as sitting snug in his own kitchen.

Born on 5th June, 1842, Scollay had been introduced to the sea at an early age by his father Willie, who was a well-respected sixareen skipper himself. In his late teens he accompanied his father on his twice-weekly trips to the far haaf, the fishing grounds forty and more miles from land, mainly to the west of Shetland where the continental shelf drops from one hundred to six hundred fathoms over the distance of two or three miles. The haaf fishing had been developed in the eighteenth century, and though the sixareen was an immensely sea-worthy vessel it was still an open boat, meaning that the crew would constantly be exposed to the elements, sunshine or storm, for the duration of the trip which would sometimes last for several days. They were looking for some of the bigger, deep sea species such as cod, ling and halibut and each boat would play out several miles of line from the boat reaching down into the depths.

Grandfather Scollay, aged 28, 1870.

Scollay soon became disenchanted with this way of life and so, following the age-old tradition of young Shetland men, he set out for the Scottish mainland ports to secure work on a merchant trader. Once in amongst the sea-faring fraternity he soon learnt that the best pay was to be found on the whaling ships, though conditions were hard and the trips normally hazardous. He signed on a whaler bound for the northern seas around Greenland, and though he thrived in the harsh working conditions he decided by the mid-1860s that he would like to experience warmer climes. He then went to work for the merchant service proper, spending the next ten years travelling to exotic destinations as far apart as the Indian colonies and the South Pacific, rounding both the Cape of Good Hope and Cape Horn several times each, and rising to the rank of bosun due to his expert seamanship, industrious nature and the respect afforded him by the rest of the crew. Eventually, though, he felt he had seen enough, and in the mid-1870s returned to Burrafirth to become skipper of a sixareen.

Things progressed well for Scollay at the haaf fishing until one particular day in July 1881 when the crew had set out in good weather after a storm had passed, with clear skies, good visibility and nothing more than a fresh breeze blowing. The weather held as they reached the fishing grounds and shot their lines, though Scollay thought the air seemed to hang heavy about them. With no other indication of an impending deterioration in the weather, they carried on laying their lines. They were fishing alongside a number of other boats from different parts of the islands, all crewed by men who felt a strong affinity with both the sea and their fellow fishermen.

Late in the afternoon, however, a dark line appeared on the horizon, the skies darkened, the sea blackened and began to heave beneath them, and the wind turned from an easy breeze into a thundering, battering juggernaut, churning the ocean into an undulating frenzy. Some of the nearby boats were obviously experiencing difficulty in maintaining a course, though most were hidden by the sheets of rain now falling in a deluge, and some appeared to have cut their lines and were making for home. Scollay was determined not to lose his lines and held the boat facing steadfastly into the wind while the crew hauled them aboard, much to the consternation of some of the younger, less experienced members aboard. With that job complete Scollay waited his moment to turn the boat back to face east and with the small reefed sail raised looked to ride the face of the storm, and outrun the worst of the weather.

As the sail caught its first gust of the howling wind the boat lurched forward and picked up speed, its thirty-foot length virtually planing across the water with the bow raised high. Despite making nine to ten knots the journey seemed endless to those on board, the craft being buffeted from all sides and in constant danger of being capsized. At the helm, Scollay knew that tacking was out of the question, as to stall side-on to these waves just once would spell disaster, so he held her to as constant a course as possible with the storm biting at their heels. The pressure on the tiller was tremendous, so to minimise the chance of it being torn from his grip he lashed his steering hand to it with one of the sheets, knowing that he would probably not get a chance to relax his hold until landfall. With the headlong speed of their progress through the waves it wasn't long before land was in sight, but Scollay knew that they were still far from safe. The currents around Unst could be treacherous even in fair weather, so he knew that laying a course across them in order to make a direct approach to land would be another likely path to disaster. With this in mind he let the island slip past him, then when he was past the worst of the currents and was in the lee of the land he finally felt that the weather had calmed enough to turn the boat and head for the shore.

By the time they finally put their feet on dry land once again the sturdy boat had endured several hours of being driven before one of the fiercest and most destructive storms of the century. Twenty-six boats had been out on the water that day, and only sixteen returned. Ten boats had foundered with the loss of fifty-eight men, six of the boats originating from Gloup, a small community in North Yell that gave its name to the tragedy. The Unst crew thanked God almighty for their deliverance from the waves, and counted themselves blessed that Scollay was their skipper and that the strength of his arm had held out against the power of the tempest. He no longer had any feeling in his hand, and when he tried to rise from his position in the stern the crew noticed that the rope that tied him to the tiller had cut through the flesh to the bone itself, and one of them had to cut him free before he himself could set foot on the shore. The knife had to be used again in order to prise the rope from his lacerated hand and once this was removed he rinsed his hand in the sea to clean the wound as best he could, then wound it about with strips of cloth they kept in the boat to act as an impromptu dressing.

The wives and families of the crew had gathered together as they realised that this was no ordinary storm. They had prayed for the safe return of their husbands, fathers, sons and brothers, and were overcome with relief when they finally made their way home. In the morning others arrived from Haroldswick, relatives of another boat crew that had not yet arrived home, to ask if Scollay and his men had seen anything of them, but they had to reply in the negative as the seas had been mountainous, the sky black, and it had taken all their concentration to bring their own boat safely back to shore. At this news Scollay was all for calling the crew together and taking the boat back out to search for the missing men, but overnight his hand had swollen to twice its normal size and had turned a putrid colour, so he was persuaded to see a doctor first. The local doctor at Baltasound, though a good man, was not thought knowledgeable enough to deal with an injury as severe as this, and as a well-known young doctor from Fetlar who had qualified as a surgeon was at this time home on holiday, Scollay decided to make his way to the neighbouring island to seek his help.

William Watson Cheyne was a twenty-eight year old who had graduated in both medicine and surgery at Edinburgh University in 1875, and was now working as house surgeon at Kings College London, under Joseph Lister, the founder of British antiseptic medicine. He had not travelled home expecting to need to use the skills of his vocation whilst visiting his family, and so had very few surgical instruments available to deal with the badly damaged hand that was now presented to him by the sturdy Unst-man. Nonetheless he would not turn an injured man away, and operated immediately with whatever implements he could find in his doctor's travelling case. The wound was still raw and Watson recognised the danger of infection setting in if not treated immediately. By the time he had finished Watson was pleased with how the operation had progressed, believing that he had saved the hand and that Scollay would retain full use of its functions. To be safe, though, he advised Scollay to travel to Edinburgh when he next had the opportunity, to attend the infirmary where Watson's work could be appraised and a further check for infection could be made. Watson waved aside Scollay's offer of payment for his treatment, though the latter pressed him to allow him to make some recompense. Scollay didn't realise at this time that the doctor would normally charge his wealthy patients fifty guineas for such a procedure, a figure far beyond the financial capabilities of a poor fisherman.

Watson would go on to have an illustrious career, well known as a pioneer of antiseptic surgical techniques and operating on many well-known figures including John Brown (of Queen Victoria fame) and King Edward VII. As well as his work at Kings College he was also consulting surgeon to the British military in the Boer War and consulting surgeon to the Royal Navy in the First World War. He was a Fellow of the Royal Society, President of the Royal College of Surgeons, served as an MP from

1917 to 1922 and Lord Lieutenant of Orkney and Shetland from 1919 to 1930 and was made a Baronet in 1908. Scollay could not have been in better hands; within a week he was back out skippering his sixareen, as there were no welfare payments to help feed your family back then if you were sick or injured, so the only thing to do was to get straight back to work as soon as you were fit enough.

Scollay's feat of seamanship in bringing his boat and crew home safely in such appalling conditions cannot be overestimated. Losing men at sea was a regular occurrence back then, and in fact only fifteen years before the great storm Scollay's cousin, my namesake Thomas Mathewson, had drowned only a few hundred yards from the safety of Baltasound harbour when his boat, carrying a load of salt fish, had foundered in a heavy sea. Thomas was the son of Scollay's uncle Joseph, who had gained fame, and later notoriety, by scaling the Hermaness cliffs in 1843 and killing the last sea eagle in Shetland on its nest. The bird's body had then been presented to the laird to be stuffed and displayed in his library, and Joseph's reward had been a sack of flour, scant recompense perhaps for the extinction of a magnificent native species.

Scollay's father, Willie, had himself had a lucky escape whilst in charge of a sixareen thirty years before Scollay's adventure. He was returning home from the haaf in July, 1851, with a full load of fish, when he misjudged the strength of the west-running current whilst attempting to pass to the east of the Outstack under sail. The Outstack is the most northerly tip of Britain, being a sizable rock, eighty feet high, lying to the north of the entrance of Burrafirth and a half-mile north-east of Muckle Flugga. The strength of the current swept the heavy sixareen up onto the eastern side of the rock as if it were no more than a child's toy, and Willie immediately ordered his crew to abandon ship, fearing that the boat would either be turned over or smashed into driftwood. They managed to scramble straight onto the rock, all except one who could not move quickly enough due to a severe disability in one leg. As swiftly as he had scrambled out, Willie leapt back into the boat as the next wave started to draw it back off the rock and into the sea, not being one to stand aside and watch his crewman being drawn to his fate alone. By good fortune the boat had not been holed or swamped by the sea, and by using a couple of oars they managed to keep her from being thrown onto the rock once more until the current had pushed them south of the Outstack and then rapidly conveyed them westwards. As the mast had been broken in the initial impact all the two crewmates could do was to attempt to row towards safety, but this was impossible at the moment due to the strength of the current, so they relaxed and saved their own strength for what might lie ahead.

Their four crewmates, meantime, had scrambled to the top of the Outstack in order to keep sight of the swiftly disappearing sixareen and to hopefully attract any passing boats to come to their rescue. They had not been fishing alone at the haaf, and they knew that it would probably not be long until some of their comrades heading home came within earshot. What they hadn't reckoned on, however, was the strength of superstition amongst fishing folk. One of the superstitions of the time was, amazingly enough, that it was unlucky to rescue anyone from the sea, and sure enough the first boat that happened past stuck to their beliefs and carried on towards home, despite hearing the cries of their neighbours. The next boat, however, skippered by Sandy Priest, defied their fears and pulled in close to the Outstack, transferring all the stranded men onto their boat. They then set out in search of Willie and his companion, eventually overtaking them more than ten miles west of where they had started. Now reunited with its full complement of crew, the sixareen was rowed back to Burrafirth and safety, Sandy following them and keeping a watchful eye on those he had saved. As a postscript to this story it is interesting to learn that rather than be blessed with good fortune for sticking so rigidly to their superstitious beliefs, the crew of the boat that originally ignored the marooned fishermen met with their own tragedy not long after. They were all of one family named Winwick, and most were lost at sea themselves when their fourareen (a four-oared boat) foundered at the fishing that next winter, an event so profound that the name Winwick then disappeared from Unst entirely.

If fishing was a hard life, then crofting was little easier. In fact, to a young man of my disposition, it was decidedly more unappealing. Farming then had not changed appreciably in hundreds of years, and was manual-labour intensive; there were no tractors in Unst at that time in the 1920s and 1930s, and at Buddabrake we didn't even have a horse to help with the heavy work. We would work in the fields from dawn until dusk, some days turning over five acres of soil using only hand-spades, which was back-breaking work and not at all to my liking. More often than not my brothers would turn a blind eye to their youngest sibling, as after lagging well behind them for the first part of the day I would fetch the shotgun and sneak off on the pretext of bagging a few rabbits. I wasn't a bad shot back then, and working with the ferret would usually end up with several for the pot. There were always plenty of rabbits around, the easiest ones to find living

Thomas Mathieson (foreground) cutting hay with Johnny Christie, 1937.

in burrows on the sand flats between the loch and the sea, and my mother's rabbit stew was always a welcome supplement to the usual fare. As I have mentioned, crofting in those days was hard toil, and not, unfortunately, suited to my temperament. I persevered with it, though always hoping that some other employment opportunity would present itself locally. It never did, just the odd casual job occasionally, which would barely earn me enough to keep me in cigarettes and pay my two shillings entrance at the local whist-drive and dance.

There were three halls on Unst, at Haroldswick, Baltasound, and Uyeasound in the south where the dances would become the focal point for the community, especially over the long, winter months when the lack of daylight hours meant only a limited amount of time could be spent working. The dancing would go on from seven in the evening until three in the morning, though quite often the young men would spend a lot of the time congregated together at one end of the hall, sharing a dram of whisky or rum from a "flattie" (half-bottle) and a laugh or two. This was not so much due to shyness but rather the knowledge that no right-minded single girl would be interested in a man with so few prospects, as was I, with no proper employment.

The dances were a welcome distraction, but most socialising and entertainment was homemade and home-based for the greater part of the year. Once the day's work was over my mother and sisters would prepare the evening meal, prior to which there would often be a tap on the kitchen door and one or two of the neighbours would peer into the warm glow of the kitchen. They would always be welcomed in to share the meal, and

Sunday best with mother and Jimmy Andrew (right), Burrafirth, 1938.

Jimmy Andrew, mother and Ann Tamar, 1933.

then would afterwards repay their hosts with a story or two, or perhaps a tune and a song. Like most Shetland folk we made our own "hom bru", and there would always be a barrel standing in one corner of the kitchen, adding its own very distinctive smell to the cornucopia of odours. There would normally be a musician present (my brother Johnny was a fine fiddle player), and the potent mix of good company, music and alcohol would see the rugs kicked to one side of the room and the reels begin. I can't say the dancers ever appeared too light on their feet, as most would be wearing heavy working boots, but that wouldn't impede their speed or enthusiasm and quite often pieces of furniture or even younger members of the throng would find themselves catapulted by an accidental stray boot to join the rugs on the sidelines.

Despite being surrounded by a loving family and living in a home that usually reverberated with music and laughter, at the age of twenty I decided that enough was enough, crofting was not for me, that it was time to move on from the life I had known up until now, time to find out what was waiting over the horizon.

BORN A BEACHCOMBER

Chapter Three

It was a fine spring day in 1938 when my brother Johnny and I finished a hearty breakfast, took our leave of a tearful mother and swung our canvas holdalls over our shoulders to start our long journey south, away from the only life I had known up until then.

We were both in good spirits, though Mother had not taken the news that I was leaving well at all; there must be very few mothers who do not feel a sense of loss when their youngest child packs his things and leaves home, particularly when they will be putting an ocean between themselves and their family. Perhaps on this occasion there was more than simple motherly worry showing on her anxious face, as the world we two were stepping forward to face was growing more uncertain with every passing day. For several years now Germany's resurgence as a world power had been making the headlines, accompanied lately by ever more bold and aggressive rhetoric; even we on a speck of an island in the North Sea could see that this new political ideology, fascism, national socialism or whatever they called it, was threatening to destabilise the old order of things in Europe. War, though, was another thing altogether, and at that time quite unimaginable, as we were led to believe that the French army could not be matched on land, whilst the oceans of the world were patrolled by the most powerful fleet the world had ever known – the British Royal Navy. How could a comical-looking little dictator whose army went on manoeuvres in cardboard tanks, so we were told, be a threat to the kind of firepower that could be assembled by these two great and powerful nations?

Worries of this nature were certainly not at the forefront of our minds that morning as sauntered down the Buddabrake road on our way to Baltasound, the main settlement in Unst, which lay on the far side of Setters Hill and was until recently one of the centres of the seasonal herring industry in the north of Scotland. Both my mother and my sister Anne had worked as gutter lasses, gutting and packing the "silver darlings" into barrels, as had most of the able-bodied Unst girls of the time. Baltasound had been a boom-town in the early days of the twentieth century, the industry turning it from a township with a normal population of five hundred to a swarming community of ten thousand, boasting six hundred boats operating from forty-eight different herring stations around the bay. Baltasound had seen its heyday by the time of the First World War and by now the old herring industry was disappearing as fast as it had arrived.

The sun was shining, reflecting brightly from the pools of peaty water dotted around the heather moors and the grassy meadows, whose fragrance combined with a fresh breeze and gave us a feeling of strength and well-being as we struck out along the track. At Baltasound pier we boarded the mail boat, an old steamer that would carry us to Lerwick, Shetland's capital. In these days of easy and convenient travel it is hard to imagine that travelling from the north of Shetland to the south would be any great

Unst gutter lasses. From left –back: Mima Anderson, Baba Mathieson, Bena Margaret Thomson, Marion Thomson, Willa Thomson, Minnie Gray. Middle: Liza Charlotte Anderson, mother (Doya), Hariot Thomson, Mary Laureson, Balantine Anderson. Front: Aggie Thomson, unknown, Lizzie Priest.
(Courtesy of Claire Auty and Unst Heritage Centre)

hardship, but there were no such things as roll-on roll-off ferries back then and ahead of us lay several hours steaming.

After spending a few hours in Lerwick and purchasing our tickets south, we boarded the ship that would take us on the next leg of our journey that same evening. We arrived in Aberdeen the following morning after a twelve hour crossing, from where we took a train to Edinburgh and finally a bus to Leith docks. This was my first trip south without one or both of my parents, and Leith in those days was a busy port, with countless numbers of little fishing smacks stacked up five abreast at their jetties, alongside steamships busy loading or unloading cargo, some arriving and some preparing to depart. I was fascinated by the comings and goings, the frenetic activity, the shouting of the dock workers, the clanking of chains and the whirring of cranes, the smells of fish and diesel oil mingling to create a potent dockside aroma.

Johnny had more important things on his mind than the commercial machinations of Leith docks, and soon dragged me towards the nearest hostelry to sample what liquid refreshment they had to offer. I had never been inside an actual pub before, having only drunk alcohol at home or at the local dances, and the word "saloon" above the bar entrance conjured up all sorts of exciting possibilities to someone who had enjoyed cowboy novels as a child. I was a little disappointed to find only one old chap sitting at the bar, who nodded our acquaintance then quickly returned to servicing his pipe, a few tatty-looking tables and chairs, a well-used dart board and a bored-looking barman. The beer tasted fine though, dark and heavy, with a thick frothy head which clung to the sides of the glass like warm butter, and soon enough the aching limbs and stiff joints from the journey south were forgotten. My brother had secured a position on a ship before leaving home, and was to meet it in Leith this day. He was excited about the prospect of getting to sea again, as this was not his first trip, and after a couple of hurried pints said "Well Tam, this is where we part company. Keep your wits about you when you're in the docks and at sea, and don't forget to write home and let the folks know what you're up to occasionally."

With that we paid our tab, picked up our belongings and went out onto the street, where we stood blinking in the bright sunlight after the gloomy interior of the pub. A quick handshake, a nod of the head and I was watching Johnny's back as he crossed the road in the direction of the dock, finally turning a corner and disappearing from sight. In contrast to my well organised brother I had left home with the vague intention of securing employment once I was on the mainland, as I had seen his imminent departure south as the ideal opportunity to cut loose from home but still have some company as I set forth.

My cousin Bella was living in Leith at that time, her husband Willie working at the dock gates checking the cargoes in and out. I knew she would be pleased to see me, as she hadn't been back to Unst for several years and would be keen to catch up on all the gossip and comings and goings. I had their address written on a scrap of paper, so set off in search of the house. One thing I hadn't anticipated, though, was the difficulty of finding an address in a town; until now my world had consisted of beaches, fields of grass and heather, the waters of Burrafirth and a few croft-houses clustered around the north-end of Unst.

I had once travelled to Aberdeen when I was twelve years old, to see my father, but of course had not been left to navigate the streets alone. As I have said, Father had been a crofter and fisherman, but only through the summer months. When the bright yellow days of summer turned to the deep golden hue of autumn, the harvest was brought in, the animals had been to sale and the days began to grow perceptibly shorter, Father would spend a day in the barn, preparing the tools of his winter trade. The meagre amounts of money we could raise in those days by the sale of our lambs, a little produce and occasionally a haul of fish certainly helped with our mainly subsistence existence, but was not enough to sustain our family over the harsh winter months. So in September Father would take down his canvas roll of knives, hung high in the rafters of the barn to keep small, prying fingers away from the razor-edged blades and carefully take out each one in turn, rubbing them down to take off any rust, sharpening them until each one could split a hair down the middle, and finally oiling them and replacing them in the roll.

Once this ritual was complete, he would gather us all in the kitchen for a last night together as a family while Mother made sure we all ate as good a meal as she could assemble. When I was young I would join the girls in crying on these occasions, although I would soon become distracted, as is the way with young children, and would have almost forgotten the upset by the next evening. Mother and the older boys would not cry, but bore Father's upcoming departure with moist eyes and set mouths, realising how vital this cash contribution was to the continued well-being of the family. By seven-thirty all the children would be packed off to bed, leaving our parents to sit by the cooker in the faded light of an old gas lamp, Mother knitting and Father smoking, not conversing but enjoying each other's company for the last time in a while.

By the time the house began stirring in the morning, Father would be gone, and we all knew it would be many months before we set eyes on him again. During the winter months working as a fish-splitter on the dockside in Aberdeen workers such as my father were considered skilled labour, and those more dextrous and quick with their knives could command a premium rate of pay, although of course it was still a pittance. So for a few pounds a week Father would work with fish of all species and sizes, deftly opening the wet, slippery body and removing the spine, working usually in cold and damp conditions, up to his elbows in stinking, bloody gore for up to sixteen hours a day. And when the day's work was over he would return to a damp, mildew-infested room in a rundown tenement in the backstreets of the city, where he would fall immediately into an exhausted slumber, dreaming of his cosy bed back home, his warm kitchen and his loving wife and children, before waking with the dawn to begin the routine all over again. When Mother and I arrived for a visit we saw none of this, as we had arranged to stay with a relation who was a lighthouse keeper in Aberdeen, with Father taking a weekend off and joining us there. This employment of his was certainly what kept us from destitution during the harshest months, and was no different from what many men had to endure back then to support their families, but came at the cost of his long-term health, as the long hours spent in freezing conditions meant the cold seeped into his very bones.

As his sons grew older and more capable of running the croft by themselves, Father took to spending more and more of the year at his work in Aberdeen, simply because the income was so sorely needed. Five months became seven, seven became ten, until eventually he hardly came home at all. Mother accepted the situation as did we all, crofters families' being practical, self-dependent units back then, and, as mentioned, we all understood the necessity. By the time I had reached my teenage years I would only see my father once or twice a year, on one of his fleeting visits, though we always tried to make the most of the short spells we had together.

After several wrong turns through the narrow, winding streets I found myself on the front step outside Willie and Bella's little terraced cottage, tapping on the glass pane in the front door. Bella greeted me like a long-lost son, taking me in and sitting me in an armchair in the best room, putting the kettle on the stove and bringing in a tray of cold meat and bread, followed by cakes and scones. By the time I arrived Willie was already home from his work, but he had to take a backseat as Bella was as eager as I had anticipated to hear all the news from home, and it was an hour of close questioning before he was allowed to drag me out of the door, heading for my second pub visit of the day. This one was no more like a wild west saloon than the first, but the beer was still good.

Bella was waiting with a fine supper of lamb and boiled potatoes when we returned, with a last dram of whisky to follow, after which I fell gratefully onto the bed to which I was led. The walls of the spare room in the Victorian cottage began to close in around my head as I laid myself down, and as sleep enveloped me my last thought was a hope that it wouldn't take me too long to secure employment, as I certainly didn't want the little money I had running out, leaving me having to creep back home, already a failure.

I awoke early to the unfamiliar sounds of the town shaking off its torpor and preparing itself for the day's business. With no trace of a sore head from the previous night's conviviality (it would be many years yet before I experienced my first hangover as I seemed able to recover from a drinking bout quicker than most), I finished the generous breakfast prepared for me by my cousin in the little kitchen, gave them my thanks and farewells, and set off for the docks and, hopefully, work. My intention was to scout the area first, taking note of what ships were moored up, then to methodically work my way through them, starting with those that I most liked the look of. By the time I had marched to the docks through the bright morning sunlight, I was disappointed to find that the choice was a little more straightforward than I had hoped for, as there was only one ship still remaining in port, the *Tolsta Head*, a small coaster of approximately five hundred tons. The rest had sailed in the night, while the ships now approaching the harbour to replace them would need time to off-load their cargoes and probably not be ready to sail for several days at least.

There was nothing else for it, so I approached the little merchantman with the same trepidation, I remember, as I used to feel when approaching Mr Taylor's room at school. I walked the gangplank on the upward journey, not yet the condemned man, and was pointed in the direction of the captain's cabin. I tapped on the wooden door and was immediately called in by a tired sounding voice, which did nothing to raise my hopes. Once inside however, I found the skipper to be a pleasant enough man, although not over-given to smiling unnecessarily, as was the way with most folk who have plied their trade around British coastal waters for half a century or more. He was an old man, as it seemed to me then, probably approaching seventy years, not tall and with a reddened, weather-beaten face and a shock of silver-white hair. When I explained my quest to him he shook his head and explained that he was only looking to take on an experienced hand.

"That's a shame," I replied, "I've travelled here all the way from Shetland to find work, and now I find there's only one ship left in the whole port."

"Shetland, you say, eh? I thought I was having trouble placing that accent of yours. Well, let's see what you know already. Can you box the compass?"

Boxing the compass is something that every Shetland boy was taught from an early age back then, and I found no trouble explaining this procedure to him. Happy with this part of my knowledge, he then produced two pieces of rope and asked me to tie four or five knots that he named, then finally to splice the rope. I managed all that asked me to do, and evidently he was satisfied that I was not totally wet behind the ears. The makeshift job interview had been completed to his satisfaction and he offered me a position as ordinary seaman there and then. I was overjoyed and accepted without hesitation, without in fact knowing where we might be headed or what we might be carrying, but that meant nothing to me in the euphoria of finding work so quickly. The skipper told me later that he had been intending to send me on my way, but decided to give me a chance when he heard that I was a Shetlander, as Shetland men had such a reputation as seafarers, and even a Shetland boy could prove to be a valuable asset on board.

We were to sail that very afternoon, as it happened, so I told the skipper that I would just have to return to the dock gates, where I had left my kitbag with Willie, and would then be ready. He asked me if I had brought my own provisions, as this would not be provided on board, and when I looked puzzled he explained that there was no cook on this ship, and each man would be expected to bring aboard food enough for a week, and be able to cook it for himself. I would also need a pair of Wellington boots, two pairs of overalls, "and of course you'll need to buy yourself a donkey's breakfast."

I had looked confused enough earlier, so I was determined not to look in any way ignorant at this strange instruction, so casually replied, "Oh I see, we've got livestock on board, then?"

Though he was not a man who smiled very much he broke into a wide grin at this, and then patiently explained that every man needed to bring his own bedding with him which would come, when purchased, in the form of a long sack stuffed with straw, hence the nickname "donkey's breakfast". There was little in the way of luxuries on a merchant ship back then, and working and living conditions had very probably changed very little since the advent of steam.

I found myself with just enough time to get ashore and make my purchases, then hurry back to the ship and help get the hatches on and battened down to make her ready for sea, before the skipper reappeared from the office with our sailing orders. Our first destination was to be Inverkeithing, just a short hop across to the north side of the Firth of Forth. So my first trip as a professional seaman ended up taking just over an hour, on a flat calm day with a pleasantly warm sun keeping us company. At Inverkeithing we loaded a cargo of stone bound for Poole in Dorset, and from there we sailed empty to London to fill the hold with bags of cement. Thus the pattern was set for the rest of my time on the *Tolsta Head*, with short, uneventful trips usually carrying heavy, dirty cargoes hither and thither around the British coast.

I was quite happy with the seagoing part of the work, as I was quickly learning my trade as OS on a merchant vessel, but the portside work was another matter entirely; as the junior member of crew it was I who had to scramble into the holds when each cargo had been unloaded and sweep them clean ready for the next. After ten minutes with the broom I would be gasping and spluttering, my hair and skin caked in dry, clinging dust, and no doubt my lungs were suffering the same fate. Such a thing as a face-mask had not been heard of back then, and the possible perils of excessive dust inhalation were not yet recognised.

It was not until we were back out at sea that I started to feel clean again, when the fresh sea breezes would cleanse me inside and out, and I would take mighty gulps of crisp, briny air to flush the memory of the filthy, choking hold. As the skipper gained a certain amount of faith in my seafaring abilities, the more I found myself being entrusted with the steering of the ship. My eyesight was keener than most and I had the strength of a youth brought up to handle the rigours of a life spent crofting and fishing. The seaman who normally undertook these duties was advancing in years, and found himself struggling more and more to keep her on course, especially when we were carrying no cargo and the ship was light, or if bad weather was causing her to pitch and roll. The wheel itself was a cumbersome, unwieldy object, akin to a cartwheel and hard to control in a heavy sea.

One day we were sailing north up the west coast of England when the weather closed in about us, and the combination of rain, wind and tide set the little ship to rearing up and twisting like a bucking bronco, the wheel spinning and unstoppable with the power of the ocean. The only solution in those circumstances was to switch to steam steering, an early and extremely crude version of power steering for ships. This worked well as far as managing the steering was concerned, as a smaller wheel inside the main one was now light as a feather to handle, and we were soon back on course. The drawback, unfortunately, was that the system was not efficient at keeping the steam within the pipe work, and before very long the entire wheelhouse was enveloped in a shroud of steam, visibility down to zero, with the coxswain dependent on shouted instructions from colleagues who were frantically wiping clear patches on the steamed up windows and peering out through the murk. The windows could not be opened, of course, as leaving the wheelhouse exposed to the elements in such a storm was only likely to make matters far worse. We dared not use the steam steering when there were other ships about because of the lack of visibility, and on those occasions two or three of us would struggle with the wheel until the storm abated, which could sometimes be for many hours at a stretch.

When I was on duty in the wheelhouse it was normally the ship's mate who relieved me for meal breaks. On one occasion, however, not long after the outbreak of war with Germany in September 1939, Billy Fraser, the galley boy, came up with a steaming hot mug of tea for me. He was an enthusiastic lad, keen to learn, and had been pestering me for some time to let him try his hand, so I reasoned that it would do no harm to let him take the wheel for a brief spell. The sea was not running too heavily, and it would let me enjoy my tea for five minutes.

"Stand at the side of the wheel here, Bill, and hold on to her as hard as you can. It won't matter if we go off course a few degrees one way or the other, but mind you don't let her take charge of you."

Billy gave me a confident grin as I carried my mug of tea over to the small table and chairs, happy that he had now been given his first proper sea-duty to perform on board. As is often the way with a first taste of responsibility, events conspired against the unfortunate rookie and I barely had time to sit down and look up from my tea before a wave took the prow of the ship off to port and sent the wheel spinning. Unfortunate Billy found himself being propelled up and over the wheel, across the entire width of the wheelhouse and smashing into one of the side windows, which shattered, disintegrating into a hail of crystal shards. I dropped the mug and made a dash for the wildly rotating wheel, having to take a chance and making a blind grab, hoping that I had the strength to hold it steady rather than finding myself with broken hands and wrist. Billy, meanwhile, had picked himself off the deck and found that he was more or less intact and, surveying the damage he had caused, decided to beat a hasty retreat from the wheelhouse. Unfortunately, as he saw me struggling with the wheel, in his panic he thought he might help me by putting the telegraph over to "Stop", which caused the *Tolsta Head*, already slewing sideways against the sea, to founder even deeper, and impossible to steer as she was now making no headway.

The next thing I heard was the sound of rapid footsteps, as the skipper came thundering into the wheelhouse, moving more like a seventeen than a seventy year old. He had been below when the ship had taken a sudden veer to port, then stopped altogether. His first assumption was that we had fallen prey to a German raider, and had hove to at their command, as in wartime nobody on board except the captain can order the ship to stop all engines. Having got to the wheelhouse and found there being no good reason why we had stopped, his first thought was to get us underway again, as, though we had not encountered any Germans as yet, the fact that we were wallowing around like a stunned whale made us a sitting duck for any who might chance our way. After the ship was moving again he turned to me.

"What do you think you're doing, Tom? You know you have no right to stop the ship!"

I had no alternative but to come clean and tell him most of what had transpired.

"Billy had just brought me some tea in, skipper, when we caught a wave and poor Bill went head over heels into the window. I rushed over to help him, thinking she'd be o.k. for a few seconds, when we got caught by another, which turned us sideways. As Bill then fell out through the door he accidentally caught hold of the telegraph, which I couldn't do anything about as I was struggling with the wheel. Bill was in a bit of a state and hopped it, and then you arrived."

I don't think he was entirely convinced by all the details in the story, and he certainly hauled me over the coals for leaving the wheel unattended, even to help a colleague who may have been injured. But the mug lying cracked on the deck, the now-cold tea-stain and the broken window spoke for themselves, and seemed to corroborate at least a part of my story. If I had admitted to allowing the galley boy to take over the steering we would probably have both been off-loaded at the next port, so I thought that a little economy with the truth on this occasion would benefit Bill as much as me. The lesson was well learnt, however, as I realised that if we had been in a convoy, or even just had another ship nearby, the consequences could have been extremely serious, as they could have been if a passing U-boat had found us while we were stalled and stationary.

Prior to the wheelhouse incident my competence as a crew member had been progressing steadily, as had my studies for the next level, Able Seaman, and whenever I found myself with any spare time on my hands I would have my head buried in books and charts. The skipper had been happy to hand me more and more responsibility as time passed and I proved myself capable, but after this I believed that there was a certain coolness in his attitude towards me, which when I look back now is understandable, given that he had believed his ship to have been in danger. Being young, though, I was a little aggrieved that he was judging me on my one error thus far, and determined that the time had come for a change.

I had been earning my living as a professional mariner for more than eighteen months now, the first flush of excitement at success in entering my chosen career so quickly had faded, and the time had arrived to evaluate my current situation against my hopes for the future. Even before my recent gaffe I had been aware of a growing frustration with the monotony of the familiar pattern of short hops between British ports, never being at sea for more than a day or two at a time, and never experiencing the glamour of mooring up in a foreign land, unless you can count Cardiff. So one evening in early November, 1939, I sat down at the end of my shift and weighed up my options for the future.

The war had been on the go for a couple of months now, and though it was being called a "phony war" by the newspapers due to the lack of impact it had had on the civilian population on land, it was certainly the real thing already for those of us plying our trade on the seaways around the UK. It appeared at this time that Hitler was simply doing a mopping-up job in the East; Poland had gone, Russia was colluding with rather than fighting Germany, and it seemed just a matter of time before the Nazi forces turned to the west. British merchant shipping was already being sunk, and even the Royal Navy was taking losses to U-boats, the most notable for me being the battleship Royal Oak. Like most young men at the time, I was keen to do my bit and get involved in the war effort before it was all over (most "experts" seemed to think it would last between six to nine months), though I knew that I did not necessarily have to leave the merchant navy to do this. In an earlier conversation the skipper had told me that we were working in what had been designated a "vital service", and explained that nothing was more important than ensuring the constant supply of raw materials and finished goods that would feed the country and maintain our capability of fighting a war. So I could combine the twin desires of wanting to serve my country and seeing more of the world by signing on with the deep-sea merchant service.

What were my chances of contact with the enemy? As far as I was concerned, a little coaster popping in and out of ports up and down the British coastline was just as likely to snag a mine or attract the unwanted attention of a U-boat as an oil tanker steaming from the Persian Gulf. For the crew of the *Tolsta Head* in particular the odds would be stacked pretty high against surviving a hit, as if we were carrying one of our usual cargoes of cement, coal or stone, it did not take much imagination to foresee that we would head for the bottom like an express train. With our next port of call being Liverpool, I decided to let the skipper know my decision right away, and then I would be able to leave the ship at a major port, enhancing my chances of finding another ship with minimal delay. I went to his cabin, and to my surprise he seemed genuinely upset at the thought of losing me. He told me that my prospects on the *Tolsta Head* were good, even of eventually running the ship, and offered to make my wages up to an Able Seaman's rate there and then.

"I'm sorry, skipper, but it's not just about the money. I really appreciate the start you've given me, but I think it's about time I saw a bit more of the world."

He realised that my mind was made up, so he signed off my log book, made up my papers and shook my hand. When we docked on the Mersey I walked down the gangway with my knapsack over my shoulder, looking forward to a new challenge, and set off for the nearest shipping agent's office.

With the raw optimism of youth I had spent my last few days and nights on the coaster dreaming of swaying palm trees, warm breezes, sultry women and the taste of rum on my lips. This was what I imagined to be waiting for me at the end of my first outbound trip on a deep sea vessel. I was still not disillusioned when I signed on with the Anchor Donaldson ship *King Idwal* heading for Varna in Bulgaria, as I had never heard of the port or the country, though I knew that we would not be sailing for tropical climes. It was enough that we would be heading for a foreign shore, and my lack of knowledge meant a nice sense of mystery. I had to travel to Cardiff to rendezvous with the ship, and found the *King Idwal* waiting for me at the dockside. She looked a good, sturdy vessel, twenty years old and at just over 5,000 tons was far larger than the old *Tolsta Head*. My feeling was that my time on the coaster had been a good apprenticeship, but my time at sea was really starting now, and I was tingling with excitement and anticipation as I walked up the gangway.

I introduced myself to the skipper, a middle-aged man this time, and with certainly not as paternal an outlook as the last. He was very business-like, with a no-nonsense attitude and very economical with words, though he took the time to explain my duties to me. The *King Idwal* was starting to load coal when I arrived, so I pitched in to help with this, and found myself once again covered in soot and dust. "Not much change here, then," I thought to myself. Although we were taking our cargo to Varna, the skipper warned me that we would not be heading straight back to Britain, as we would be loading various cargoes that were bound for the troops in North Africa, so from Varna we would be sailing south across the Mediterranean and returning via Alexandria in Egypt. That suited me down to the ground, as it was foreign lands I had signed on to see, and it sounded like I was about to see more of them in one trip than I had realised.

We left Cardiff and sailed south with the west coast of England to our port side, hugging the shoreline before heading south-west, across the Bay of Biscay, round the north-west corner of Spain, then east into the Straits of Gibraltar. The *King Idwal* steamed on an easterly heading, passing to the south of Sardinia then Sicily, before turning north through the Greek

Crew of King Idwal, *Alexandria, Egypt, 1940. (Far left with the Fez.)*

Islands to approach the mouth of the Dardanelles. We encountered no problems whilst sailing the length of the Mediterranean, mainly because at this time Italy had not entered the war. I'm sure we would have had a much hotter reception if our journey had been just six months later. By-passing Istanbul on the outward leg, we passed through the Dardanelles into the Sea of Marmara, and after navigating this were piloted through the Bosporus into the Black Sea.

We approached the harbour in Varna in the second week of December, the weather being much colder than we had imagined when we first studied the charts after learning of our destination, with a freezing north wind blowing all the way from the Baltic. As we tied up I peered through the evening twilight into the old town surrounding the port, and despite the gloom felt a thrill that I was about to take my first steps onto foreign soil. Bulgaria at that time was a neutral country, and Varna was a busy cosmopolitan town, with influences obviously from both Europe and Asia, though each bar we tried seemed to have a disproportionate number of German seamen in residence. We found ourselves in conversation with them on more than one occasion, and although they were generally a little on the arrogant side, with a lot of warnings such as "Hey, Tommy! (I was always surprised they knew my name) Don't worry about sailing home, our U-boats will help you fly back to England!" and the like, we learnt that they were all holed up here for fear of the Royal Navy.

What with discharging our shipment of coal and then loading up for the next leg, we ended up staying in Varna for three weeks, which meant celebrating Christmas in Bulgaria, before departing early in the New Year. I wasn't sure what denomination of Christians Bulgarians were, and there appeared to be Moslem influences in some of the dress and architecture, but they were certainly serious about their celebrations. The streets were festooned with bunting, a small tree was erected in a little square near the quayside, and the bars were packed with revellers. Crews from various nations indulged in a friendly, if off-key, carol-singing competition on Christmas Eve, and the singing went on in a good-humoured fashion well into the early hours of Christmas day. I had several invitations from locals to spend the day at their homes and to share their food, but we were instructed to return to the ship by lunchtime, where Christmas dinner was waiting. With the Christmas festivities over, Varna quickly slipped back into a quiet, watchful mode, with the air of a town that didn't quite know if it favoured east or west, or German, British, Russian or Turk, as I believe it had changed hands between different nationalities and creeds on several occasions in the past. The bars became quiet, and a sense of foreboding settled about the place, which was probably more to do with the times we lived in than the location, but I was glad when we secured our last loads and pushed out into the Black Sea once more.

This time we did stop at Istanbul as we headed back towards the Mediterranean, and what a contrast it was to Varna. We saw no evidence that the war had reached this Turkish peninsular and found no interest or enthusiasm for it among the general population. Sailing through the Bosporus into the harbour of The Golden Horn is an unforgettable experience for any seafarer, with the Galata Tower dominating one side of the harbour beyond the bustling Galata Bridge. Unfortunately, on closer inspection, the town itself didn't live up to its promise. Once we were clear of the paved dock area we found ourselves in a district where the streets were little more than muddy tracks, constantly churned up by an endless procession of antiquated motor vehicles and horse-drawn carts and fed by a constant drizzle. The houses were poor affairs mainly, mostly ramshackle buildings that seemed to have utilised a number of different materials in their construction, including concrete blocks, wood and corrugated iron. The people were attired in keeping with their surroundings, mostly tatty clothing covered with mud-spattered greatcoats to keep out the winter rain and cold. The going improved closer to the city centre proper where the roads were better maintained and the buildings began to reflect something of the wonderful history of the former capital of the Byzantine Empire. We lingered in the former Constantinople only long enough to see some of the main tourist sites, including the immense Hagia Sophia, built initially as a Christian church, converted into a mosque and by now a museum, and the fabled Blue Mosque with all its domes and minarets. I had never seen anything built on the scale of these two places of worship, and I must admit the architecture looked very alien to my eyes. We also visited the Grand Bazaar, which was an assault on the senses from the vivid colours of Persian carpets, pungent smells of spices, the constant cacophony of people and animals, and where everything imaginable seemed to be for sale, though after a little haggling I settled for just a very nice coffee set for my mother.

From Istanbul we sailed south to Egypt, and the port of Alexandria. This was my first time setting foot on African soil, and in very different circumstances to my next landing. The heat was incredible, even at this time of year, and I was struck immediately by the mixture of ancient and modern, and of Arab and European. Around the docks were some obviously ancient structures, massively built and beautifully crafted, with what appeared to be the flimsiest of shacks seemingly tacked onto the side, wherein you would find many generations of the same family living in the most basic conditions. The streets had open sewers, and rats feeding on the excrement would share the pathway with immaculately dressed European gents. The souk nearest the port was a lively affair, packed with goods from all around the world being sold by any number of colourful characters, and the air was full of the shouts of haggling and horse-trading. We were given two nights off to let off some steam in the local bars, where the honey wine in particular flowed freely; a little too freely for one of my shipmates, in fact, who, on exiting the bar, was struck over the head from behind and relieved of his wallet. He arrived back at the ship in the morning after sleeping it off, poorer but wiser.

After three days in Alexandria we set sail for home, and our good fortune held all the way back to Scotland, as we saw nothing of the enemy in either the Mediterranean or the Atlantic, eventually arriving in Glasgow in March 1940. The ship was now due for a refit and was therefore releasing the crew, meaning another search for work for me. The *King Idwal*, unfortunately, would not survive to the end of the war. On 17th November, 1940, she sailed from Liverpool as part of convoy OB244, which five days later was ordered to disperse due to suspected enemy presence. After just one further day's sailing the *King Idwal* was sunk by U-boat U-123 on 23rd November, with twelve of the crew, including men I had worked with, losing their lives as she slipped beneath the waves.

In Glasgow I collected my pay and caught the first train to Edinburgh, where I headed straight for Thomson's shipping office, intending to find a job and set sail again at the earliest opportunity. They had a vacancy for an A/BS on a ship of the Ben Line, namely *Ben Lomond* which was sailing from Liverpool in a couple of days. I immediately headed south for Liverpool, but when I arrived I found that the skipper had made up his full complement of crew, and they sailed the day after I arrived. It may have been a blessing in disguise, even though the *Ben Lomond* was to lead something of a charmed life for the next two years, and acquired the reputation of being a lucky ship to sail on. Consequently many of her crewmen liked to stay with her whenever and wherever she sailed, especially as so many of her sister ships had gone to the bottom.

In November, 1942 the *Ben Lomond*'s good fortune ran out, and she was sunk by U-boat U-172's torpedoes whilst en-route from Port Said in Egypt to Paramaribo in Dutch Guyana (now Surinam) and steaming 750 miles east of the mouth of the Amazon. Unfortunately she sank in a matter of minutes, and out of the 52 crew only one man is known to have survived, though later rumours were that perhaps up to eleven others were rescued. He was Poon Lim, a Chinese steward, and his story of survival was one of the most remarkable of the war. When he heard the explosion, at 11.45hrs on the morning of 23rd November, he immediately donned his life-jacket and made his way to his designated boat station. As he was helping some of his fellow crewmen to lower a lifeboat, as it was already obvious that the Ben Lomond had been fatally damaged and was starting to list, a wave washed over the deck and swept him into the sea. That wave probably saved Poon Lim's life, as he was dragged deep below the surface before his life-jacket brought him back up, and when he looked around him there was no longer a ship to be seen, just driftwood and wreckage. It is likely that at the moment he was swept overboard the ship's boilers exploded, tearing the ship apart and killing all those still trapped below decks.

Poon Lim was now alone in the ocean, clinging to one of the ship's planks in a desperate state of mind until, with amazing good fortune, he spotted a Carley life-raft bobbing in the sea a couple of hundred yard away. He managed to paddle over to it and haul himself aboard, finding its store of six large boxes of biscuits, two pounds of sugar, two pounds of chocolate, ten cans of pemmican (a concentrated mixture of fat and protein), a bottle of lime, five cans of evaporated milk and forty litres of water, intact. At this point he noticed another life-raft, with four other survivors aboard, floating some distance away. Although the occupants of the other raft hailed him, he was now exhausted, and could not find a way of propelling himself towards his fellow mariners. They were obviously in the same situation, as bit by bit the two rafts floated apart, and Poon Lim never saw them again. What he did see very clearly, though, was the U-boat that now surfaced close to him. The crew came out on deck to survey the results of their handiwork, and totally ignored the pleas for help from the lone figure sitting in the little life-raft. These were the last humans that he would see for a very long time.

Poon Lim had food and water to last him approximately fifty days, but before long he began to realise that he may well be adrift for far longer than that, so set about supplementing his rations. He caught rain water in a tarpaulin, trapped seabirds that ventured too close and fashioned a hook from a nail to catch fish. Occasionally he would spot a ship steaming nearby and even saw planes flying overhead, but nothing he could do drew their attention, and days turned to weeks, and weeks to months, with nothing but the sea around him and the sun beating down from above. Christmas came and went, 1942 turned to 1943, and it was not until 2nd April that rescue came in the form of a Brazilian fisherman who spotted the raft floating ten miles off the mouth of the Amazon River and who took the exhausted but relieved young steward aboard his vessel. It was another three days before Poon Lim finally set foot on dry land, at Belem in Brazil, one hundred and thirty days after his ordeal began. He was in remarkably good shape for a man who had spent four and a half months on the western Atlantic in an open life-raft, and the length of his epic fight for survival in such a craft is still a world record.

Though I was disappointed not to have shipped out on the *Ben Lomond* the Liverpool office assured me that they had a position for me on the next "Ben boat" sailing from Liverpool, the *Benarty*. That would be in two weeks so they gave me an address for reasonably-priced lodgings in the city, and I awaited the arrival of the ship that was to carry me to my own first-hand experience of the conflict at sea.

BORN A BEACHCOMBER

Chapter Four

The *Benarty* steamed out of Liverpool on the evening tide of 16th April, 1940, bound for Rangoon in Burma via Aden, carrying a general, mixed cargo, including a substantial amount of coal in number one hold. This was to be my first trip to the other side of the world, to a far-flung colony and an exotically-named city in a country that was the gateway to the mysterious orient. This was the voyage I had been dreaming about when I had been at the wheel of the little coastal steamer, and I was excited and ecstatic about my good fortune in finding myself on such an adventure on only my second deep-sea trip. I was even more delighted when I discovered that there were four more Shetland men onboard. I was well acquainted with Bertie Bruce from Unst, the others being two Whalsay men, Dodie Irvine and Andrew Sandison, while Johnny Cogle from Cunningsburgh was the bosun. They all had a number of year's service in the merchant marine and I knew they would be there for me to turn to if I needed advice or just to hear a friendly voice from home. They had plied the trade routes to the Far East on many occasions between them and knew what to expect both in terms of keeping the ship functioning and what awaited us at our destination.

We left Liverpool in a small convoy of eight ships, gaining speed as we left port and steaming across waves that were now red-tipped by the setting sun, escorted by a destroyer and a minesweeper before rendezvousing with the main convoy at dawn the next day. As the sun rose there were now nearly thirty ships sailing in unison for the southern oceans with half a dozen warships escorting us. As with most convoys we were an odd collection of all shapes and sizes, from long oil tankers and bulky ore carriers down to little tramp steamers of 1,000 tons. At 5,800 tons the *Benarty* was about average, not the biggest but still substantial enough to loom large as a tempting target in the periscope of any passing U-boat commander.

At this stage of the war German troops were in control of Denmark and Norway, which meant that Shetland was now as close to occupied Europe as it was to the Scottish mainland. Norway had been invaded in April 1940 and forced to capitulate two months later, even though a British taskforce had landed men and equipment to try to help the Norwegians continue their struggle. Shetland almost immediately became the centre of attempts to both extract agents and civilian refugees and infiltrate more agents into Norway, an operation that later developed into what became known as the "Shetland Bus". Initially the group operated using fishing boats, but after heavy losses these were replaced by three fast submarine hunters transferred from the US Navy, and by the end of the war hundreds of agents and refugees had been successfully transported.

Having Nazi troops virtually on our doorstep certainly gave us Shetlanders something to talk about when we were off-duty, though the main talking point in the country was the deal that Stalin had done with Hitler over annexing Poland, and there seemed to be a real possibility at that time that the two dictatorships of Russia and Germany might unite against the western democracies. We had little idea, then, that the "phoney war" was about to come to an abrupt end, and that before the next month was out the German army would show in Belgium, Holland and France that it needed no allies to fight its way to within spitting distance of the shores of England.

SS Benarty, *1940.*

The convoy headed south with fair weather and no real incidents for the first few days. The destroyers and corvettes fretted and fussed around us like so many mother ducks, scolding the stragglers into catching up and chiding those captains who allowed their ships to get too close to their neighbours. Twice, before we had even crossed the Bay of Biscay, the alarm was given that a periscope had been sighted, and the escorts would race at full steam to the area of the sighting, being a fine sight as they weaved through the plodding merchantmen at 30 knots, zigzagging frantically as they searched for a sign of the lurking predator. On the second occasion contact must have been made, as one of the ships dropped a line of depth charges astern, each of which sent a plume of white water thirty feet into the air, but obviously missed the intended target. If the submarine had been there it must have decided on discretion being the better part of valour, as the convoy resumed its course and no more enemy sightings were made. The next brief glimpse of land was Cape Finisterre once we had made the Biscay crossing, but this soon dwindled behind us as we steamed south-west until we were approximately forty miles west of the nearest landfall, at which point we resumed our heading due south.

There were no further alarms as the weather improved and the temperature rose, though once we were south of the Algarve part of the convoy peeled off to the east, heading for the Straits of Gibraltar and the Mediterranean. The main group carried on south to run parallel with the West African coast, taking the longer but hopefully less hazardous route to the Indian Ocean via the southern tip of Africa. By this time the crew had settled into a routine, and as with all long sea journeys, monotony became our primary enemy. Sailors will always welcome a distraction from the routine, and next on the agenda was "crossing the line", supposedly an initiation into "the solemn mysteries of the ancient order of the deep" for those who were passing the equator for the first time. For several days prior to the event my Shetland pals took great delight in unsettling me with lurid descriptions of how the ceremony would unfold, through various degrees of depravity, mostly involving the ship's cat, until I was a just a little unnerved.

The day of the ceremony found the four of us who were to be initiated huddled together below deck, listening to the general merriment taking place up top, until one by one we were escorted to our fate. To my relief the skipper, Captain Watt, dressed as King Neptune, explained that we were very fortunate as due to there being a war on we would only be exposed to the shortened version of the initiation. This still involved being stripped, tied to a chair, shaved by Davy Jones (played by Johnny Cogle), covered in engine grease then dunked in a large barrel of very cold seawater, but on the whole I was relieved to have got off so lightly and no doubt the cat shared the sentiment.

The journey to Rangoon via Aden took us fifty-four days in all, and though the work became tedious through daily repetition, being at war has the effect of keeping the senses keen and time passes with an anticipatory edge. For me every day was bringing a new experience.

Our escorts left us when we reached Sierra Leone, and we merchantmen were then on our own. Two or three ships detached themselves from the convoy as we made ready to round the Cape of Good Hope, heading for Cape Town. Of the remainder, half steamed on steadily for the Indian Ocean, with the other half heading north along the coast of East Africa. We were in the latter group, though we had an unscheduled stop at Durban due to a suspected fire in one the coal holds. Once we had made a close inspection and no fire was detected we resumed our journey north, though by this time the other ships had left us far behind. It was on the first morning with Africa to port that I awoke to a surprise; during a breezy night the deck had become awash with flying fish. I had heard of them before, but had had no idea that they would clear the surface of the sea by such a margin and reach the deck of a modern steamer. I picked one or two up, and as I examined them thought what a blessing my forebears would have perceived it to be if the fish at home willingly surrendered by flinging themselves into the boat, though these appeared to mostly bone and little flesh, and not at all attractive to look at. I was given the job of shovelling them over the side to make a meal for our accompanying seabirds, including one huge albatross who had attached himself to us two days before.

Unfortunately, making our acquaintance did not prove to be lucky for this particular bird, which perhaps also led in turn to a change in fortune for the ship, depending on whether you put any store in superstition or not, though most sailors do. Two days after receiving its breakfast of flying fish, and during a sudden squall, the albatross collided with the ship's rigging and crashed to the deck not far from where I was standing. Whether it had been killed outright by the collision or not I couldn't be certain, as before I could reach it one of the Chinese firemen collected the body up and disappeared below with it. What is certain is that it was taken straight to the kitchen where it was plucked and cleaned and became the main ingredient in that night's stew. This was quite an alarming development for most of the rest of the crew, as we all knew that it is bad luck to kill an albatross; the Ancient

Mariner hadn't fared too well after thoughtlessly despatching an earlier cousin. Although Chinese folk are generally among the most superstitious in the world in my experience, they obviously didn't share this particular one with their western counterparts.

As fate would have it, either by coincidence or by darker workings, that same night one of the Chinese firemen died. He went to bed a young, fit, healthy chap, and was found stone-cold dead by one of his crewmates in the morning, with no cause of death apparent. I was given the task of helping a couple of his friends dress him in his best suit, put enough rice in his pockets to sustain his spirit until it returned to his home in China, and finally sew him into a canvas sheet. The captain informed the crew of his intentions, then stopped ship and performed a proper burial at sea, the first I had ever witnessed. As for the rest of us, we exchanged nervous glances and quietly hoped that this was the end of our bad fortune and not just the beginning.

I had one further close-encounter with a Chinese crewman before we docked at Aden, this time the ship's cook. It was a hot, airless day, and I was working on deck under a cloudless sky when bosun and fellow Shetlander Johnny Cogle called for me to follow him. I fell into step behind him until we reached number two hold, where the cook was lying spread-eagled on the hatches, fast asleep in the sun and snoring like a buzz-saw. Johnny had an oil-can in his hand, and, creeping silently up to the comatose Chinaman, proceeded to pour the thick, brown liquid straight into the gaping mouth. First we heard a gurgling noise, then a choking splutter, and then a dark, viscous fountain shot into the air as the cook gagged and expelled the oil in one tremendous retching motion. I was standing back roaring with laughter at the entertainment and didn't notice Johnny place the oil-can at my feet and slip away behind the cover of the winches, when the cook started hauling himself to his feet, looking for the perpetrator. Seeing the empty oil-can and the young seaman doubled up with laughter standing next to it, the cook could only come to one conclusion. He launched himself towards me and made a grab for my head, but I had come to my senses just in time to duck, turn and take to my heels. The cook was a big man, with arms as thick as my thighs, and was literally spitting mad, so I didn't think it wise to linger and argue my innocence. With heavy footsteps in hot pursuit I dashed aft along the deck, took the bridge ladder in two giant strides, crashed unceremoniously through the captain's cabin door and slammed it shut behind me. Captain Watt had been busy writing up his log, and nearly fell off his chair with shock as I burst in.

"What the hell are you up to, Tom?" he spluttered, as I thrust a dining chair under the door handle and looked around for some heavy furniture to pile against the door.

"Sorry sir, but the cook wants to kill me!" I uttered breathlessly, with my back against the door and legs braced to keep it shut. As the skipper didn't bother asking why, and had something of a humorous twinkle in his eye, I had the idea that he had probably been watching and knew exactly what had happened, though he didn't let on.

"Open the door now, and let me sort this out" he said, taking his chair away from the handle and stepping out onto the walkway. I shut the door quickly behind him, and listened anxiously as he calmed down the irate cook, eventually persuading him to retreat to the galley after convincing him that he took the matter very seriously and would punish me accordingly. He returned to the cabin after five minutes, again with a look of suppressed mirth

"Well, he's calm enough now, but you know I don't hold with baiting the Chinese crewmen, so I'm docking you five shillings for invading my privacy, and try to leave them alone in future!"

Now five shillings was a lot of money to me then, so I'd certainly had the smile wiped off my face by the time I went below to find Johnny and give him a piece of my mind for the trouble he'd caused me. I found him still laughing about the cook chasing me around the deck, and when I told him about bursting into the old man's cabin and being fined five shillings, he laughed even harder. At this point I forgot about the money and joined in the laughter, though I was always very careful in future when I thought that Johnny might be in the mood to play one of his practical jokes.

We made it to Aden with no further trouble, sailing through a heat haze into the harbour and off-loading our precious cargo of coal bound for Steamer Point. This was an important re-fuelling point for the Royal Navy, so cargoes such as ours were vital. Aden itself seemed a place that had had most of the colour drained out of it, leaving only faded impressions of the hues they might once have been under a shimmering white-blue sky. It was like sailing into a giant amphitheatre, and Johnny told me that the town and harbour were built on the rim of an ancient, volcanic crater. You could well imagine that it had once been the haunt of pirates, but we were more concerned with avoiding the present-day German variety. Aden, despite the ancient look to the town, was a busy modern port, with ships standing off waiting for a berth to discharge their coal. This being the case we didn't stay long after being unloaded, especially as we weren't picking up any cargo for the trip home until we reached Rangoon, so we sailed the next day. I would have liked to have had a chance to look around and have a word with some of the local boys, all dressed in loose-fitting white robes and turbans, but it wasn't to be, so we made steam and headed east into the Indian Ocean.

After a journey of nearly two months that took us through the Maldive Islands we finally found ourselves in a wide estuary leading upriver to the port of Rangoon. This was now August, the middle of the rainy season, though the heat was still sticky and oppressive. The air seemed to be full of little dark flies that were determined to find a meal somewhere on your face or body, more tenacious even than Shetland midges, and the only breeze that blew was a warm one straight out of the jungle, carrying musky odours and the cries of unseen and unknown animals and birds. The city of Rangoon was out of sight beyond the port area, and in the two weeks we were moored up we had many opportunities to explore this bustling metropolis. On first reaching the city I was struck by how lush with vegetation it was and how many waterways and lakes it seemed to be built around. Palm trees and pagodas vied for space with shops and dwellings and the air always seemed sweet with the scent of flowers or incense, especially in the evenings. The short, wiry inhabitants were a friendly bunch, especially if they thought they might be able to sell you something, but generally they left you alone and carried on about their own business. There was a real mix of races and nationalities in Rangoon, with Burmese, Chinese and Indian markets frequented by south and north Europeans as well as a few Americans I got talking with.

There was also a range of architectural styles, with local structures, particularly the impressive pagodas, sitting alongside buildings which had obvious British influences. I knew virtually nothing of the history of Rangoon, but I might have taken more of an interest had I realised that my future brother-in-law, Reg Harris, would be among the first troops to march into the city to liberate it from the Japanese in just under five years, after spending several hard years fighting in the jungles of Burma.

We spent a busy fortnight loading the ship with a general cargo for the return trip, which included four hundred tons of wolfram (better known as tungsten and used for hardening steel), zinc concentrate, paraffin, tea and beans. When the ship was fully loaded the skipper took a trip ashore to receive his final sailing orders, and on his return we made preparations for sea. At this point the Chinese crew members decided that they would prefer to stay in Rangoon rather than take the chance of sailing through potentially dangerous waters back to Britain, no doubt discouraged by the many reports of shipping losses at that time in the vicinity. The skipper didn't stand on ceremony, and told them in no uncertain terms that they had signed on for a round trip, and that no-one would be leaving the ship until we reached home. Most accepted the situation as the captain explained it, but there were a couple of stokers who weren't ready to take no for an answer, and the situation was only resolved when these two troublemakers were frog-marched below and told that if they uttered one more word then they would be making the trip in irons and receive no pay. To prevent further trouble the skipper decided to bring forward the sailing by a few hours; we didn't have to wait for a convoy or escorts to gather for the homeward trip because we were travelling alone, so we sailed quietly out of harbour that night, 7th September, 1940, bound for Avonmouth and eventually Liverpool.

The first morning out dawned bright and fresh, though by midday the weather had become patchy, with frequent rain showers. Visibility would be several miles one minute, and then down to a few hundred yards the next, which kept us on edge. There had been reports of German raiders operating in the Indian Ocean circulating before we left Rangoon, so the skipper had decided on a route which took us farther south than a ship would normally travel when heading from Rangoon to the southern tip of Africa, hoping to avoid trouble by staying out of the usual shipping lanes. The first day and night passed uneventfully, and by lunchtime on the second day the crew had relaxed into its routine. The atmosphere on board returned to its previous tense state, however, when the early afternoon brought a wireless distress signal from a ship ahead of us, informing us that she was under attack from an unidentified raider. Our wireless operator wasted no time in attempting to pass the message on, firstly to the radio station on Mauritius, then to Natal in South Africa, but we received no reply from either. After failing to make contact with any shore-based station, the operator then broadcast a coded message on an open frequency which we hoped would alert any British warships nearby of the presence of a German raider in the vicinity.

After the initial three distress calls the radio went silent, and nothing more was heard from the unfortunate victim. The ship was actually the *Athelking*, a 9,557 ton tanker out of Liverpool, owned by the United Molasses Company. She had been steaming for the Cape when she had sighted what appeared to be another merchantman approaching, closing rapidly. The captain of the *Athelking* was initially suspicious of the stranger, so he had turned onto the same course as her in order to try to keep his distance, and had manned the small "pom-pom" gun at the stern of the tanker. The newcomer didn't react to this manoeuvre, but held his original course. At this the *Athelking*'s skipper relaxed a little, standing down his gun-crew and turning to pass astern of the other ship and thereby regain his original course. Unfortunately within minutes the other "merchantman" dropped his disguise, exposing his guns and opening fire from only 6,800 yards range. After taking several direct hits things were looking grim for the *Athelking*, when suddenly she was given a glimpse of salvation. The raider's helm had jammed, and she swung momentarily out of control. This gave the *Athelking*'s skipper, Captain Tomkins, the opportunity to man his gun, and get a blow in on the enemy. Unfortunately the three shots they managed to fire were off target; the raider came back under control, and the *Athelking* was pounded into submission. Three men were killed, including the captain, and thirty-seven prisoners were transferred to the raider before the tanker was shelled again and sent to the bottom.

Of course we didn't know any of this at the time, but we would be filled in on the details from some unexpected new shipmates in the near future. I happened to be on the bridge when the distress signals came in, and I remember the skipper agonising over whether we should change course to avoid the raider. In the end the decision was made to carry on as we were, as logic dictated that because the raider's victim had managed to transmit a distress signal, the raider's location would now be assumed to be compromised, and her captain would be keen to steam her out of the locale with all haste. The officers all agreed with the captain's rationale, but nonetheless a keen look-out was kept for the rest of the day. As day turned to night and the protective darkness closed in around us I stood on the fore-deck peering into the gloom ahead of us, unwilling to take to my bunk until the last possible moment, not wanting to tempt fate by presuming we were now safe. But the night passed much the same as the previous one, as did the following morning, until it was time for my next watch to start at midday.

Although the crew was outwardly calm and carrying on about its normal business, there was a nervous undercurrent running through the ship's company, which was reinforced by orders from the Admiralty received that morning to post extra lookouts. As I arrived on deck for duty the chief officer approached me:

"Tom, your eyesight is as good as anyone's on board; get up to the crows-nest double-quick, shout out if anything appears on the horizon and look out for periscopes."

"Aye aye, Chief," I replied confidently, though I hoped that the enemy had cleared well out of the area by now. On a fine day lookout duty in the crow's-nest on the fore-mast is not the most onerous of tasks, and I passed a pleasant hour until at 1pm I spotted a tiny speck of cloud on the horizon, approximately 10 degrees to starboard. I immediately reported the sighting to the bridge.

"OK Tom. We can't see anything ourselves yet, but see if you can make out any details."

After 10 minutes I could make out the masts and top superstructure of a vessel of some sort coming up over the horizon, and could tell that it was on a converging course with the Benarty, though probably still over twenty miles away. On receiving this information the skipper decided on evasive action, and I felt the ship beneath me heeling over slightly as we turned to port and took a heading due north. Making steam for all we were worth, I watched with some relief as the unknown ship receded over the horizon, appearing to take an avoiding course himself once he had apparently spotted us. The weather was beginning to turn now, with a few dark clouds appearing and the wind picking up, and after a half-hour or so running in a northerly direction the skipper felt confident enough to turn us back to our original heading.

Just five minutes after we had resumed our course, however, I picked up the mystery vessel once more, a little closer this time, having been hidden from view previously by a rain squall. As I reported once more to the bridge I kept the binoculars pressed to my face, and was astonished and a little perturbed to see what could only be an aircraft rise up through the rain haze about the ship, pointing it's propeller in our direction as it gained altitude.

"They're not on their way over for tea and biscuits! There's nothing more you can do up there, Tom," the chief said to me as I relayed this latest development, "Get yourself down pronto and find some cover."

I didn't need any further encouragement to vacate my exposed position, and quickly slipped out of the crow's-nest and scrambled towards the deck. Halfway down the mast I came across Johnny Cogle sitting in the bosun's chair making some repairs. I swiftly appraised him of the situation and he swung himself out of the chair and joined me in my descent. As I reached the bottom of the mast I could hear the steady droning of the plane's engine growing louder, like an approaching swarm of angry wasps. My feet hit the deck and I was off towards the bridge at full pelt, with Johnny puffing and panting hot on my heels. I reached the bottom of the ladder and risked a quick glance over my shoulder, just in time to see the plane commence his first strafing run. He had flown ahead of us and turned to attack the *Benarty* head on, no doubt to heighten the dramatic impact and encourage a swift capitulation. We were racing for cover when all hell broke loose around us. From above came the roaring of the plane's motor and the deafening clatter of its machine-guns, whilst all around bullets were raining down, ricocheting noisily off the deck and the surrounding superstructure and pinging in all directions.

Despite the pandemonium all around and the sharp "fizz" as bullets whizzed past my ears I kept running, desperate for cover, as I knew flinging myself down flat on the deck would be no protection from guns being fired from above. It was at this point that I heard Johnny cry out in pain from somewhere behind me. I had no time to look back, though, as at the same time a shipmate who was running in front of me also cried out and fell forward to the deck. I immediately thought he had been shot dead, but as I reached him he looked up and thrust an arm towards me. I grabbed the proffered hand and, without stopping, dragged him with me until we reached the lee of some cargo strapped to the deck, behind which I caught my breath and inspected my shipmate's wounds more closely. He had blood seeping into his shirt on his back and at his side, but when I pulled it open to see the extent of the wounds I quickly saw that they were only superficial. He had been peppered by small fragments of shrapnel, none of which had penetrated deeply, though they hurt badly enough for him to think he had been seriously injured. I quickly helped him clean up the wounds and left him getting his breath back under cover of the cargo and out of harm's way for the time being.

I continued making my way aft, as I was keen to find out what had happened to Johnny. Although he had cried out just before the man in front of me fell, he had then overtaken me whilst I was dragging the other to safety. Johnny had also reached cover safely, though when I found him he was holding his hand to a nasty-looking wound on his head. I managed to find a drop of water and a towel, whilst another of the boys appeared with a clean bandage, and between us we cleaned the wound and dressed it. Once again, to my surprise, the wound was not serious, just a grazed scalp and Johnny was soon on his feet and insisting he was fine. Obviously I had been lucky, as the bullets and shrapnel had straddled me, taking down both the man in front of me and the man behind, and leaving me unscathed. It was not to be the last time that I appeared to have a guardian angel looking after me.

During this time spent looking after my injured shipmates, the seaplane, a Heinkel HE 114, was pressing home its attack with great determination. For twenty-five minutes it carried on strafing the ship, turning in great, wide arcs once it had completed each run, gaining height from which to swoop down on us once more, much like the bonxies at home which will dive relentlessly at any unwary traveller who has strayed too close to their nest-site. In reality the machine-gunning did little damage, but it certainly had a strong nuisance-value, preventing us from running the ship properly. The pilot's orders had been to try to disable the radio antenna first to stop us sending warning transmissions on the radio, either by catching the antenna that was strung between two masts with a trailing hook or by shooting up the wireless room. The plane also dropped two 110lb bombs during the attack, but either a lack of accuracy on the part of the pilot or the skill of the evasive manoeuvres undertaken prevented either from finding its target, each raising a plume of water as it detonated in the sea some distance from the ship.

All during the aerial attack the ship's radio officer had been broadcasting "QQQ, attacked by raider," managing to transmit this and the ship's position a number of times before he was forced to give up by direct attacks on the radio cabin. The radio officer's diligence, unfortunately, proved to be of little help to us in our predicament, as there were no British warships in the vicinity to come to our aid.

Kneeling by Johnny and helping him to secure his dressing, another sound brought my attention to the latest development. Our gun suddenly commenced firing from the stern of the ship, so I swiftly went all the way aft to see for myself what was happening and perhaps lend a hand with the gun. Peering through the rain that was falling more steadily now, I saw that our mystery vessel was now only about two miles off, and the chief had organised a gun crew at the *Benarty*'s sole weapon to see if we could get a blow or two in ourselves. Four times our gun barked, but each time the shell landed harmlessly short, sending up a small plume of spray before the curtain of rain hid our enemy from sight and brought a halt to the firing.

The seaplane had also ceased its attack now, and I saw it head off into the low cloud in the direction of our attacker. The skipper had turned us away from our pursuer, and for ten minutes, as I kept watch at the stern, I thought that the conditions might have come to our rescue and the other had lost us in the gloom. To my disappointment this hope proved premature, as the other's prow reappeared through the rain which was now easing off, and from the guns which were now prominent on her decks it was obvious that we were up against a well-armed raider. I had only been tracking her for a minute or so when there were two flashes from the muzzles of her forward guns, followed after by a distant report, a noise not dissimilar to a locomotive passing through a station, then two large spouts of water rising from the sea a hundred yards astern of us. The raider was no more than three thousand yards behind us now and closing steadily. I made my way to the bridge to get new orders from the chief and to find out what the skipper's plan of action was. I could see little hope for us unless the weather worsened spectacularly, but at this point we were still making headway and no shells had landed on the ship, though I heard them passing overhead and landing noisily around us. As I reached the bridge I looked down to the main deck, and saw a group of figures huddled together, gesturing energetically to one another and obviously in a state of agitation. I recognised them as the Asiatic members of the crew, and, though I didn't realise it at the time, their presence on deck was to seal our fate and that of the ship. The main effect of the attack from the air, unfortunately for us, was the panic sown amongst the Chinese stokers. Once they heard the reverberations of bullets rattling on the funnel and the deep, compressive thuds as the bombs exploded next to the ship, they were convinced that the *Benarty*'s time was up, and nothing could be done to persuade them to stay at their posts. As they made for the deck the boilers lost pressure and the engines eventually crawled to a halt, and the last chance of out-running our pursuer vanished.

On the bridge I reported to the skipper that the stokers were all on deck and at that moment the engines started to slow and our forward momentum began to stall.

"OK boys, there's nothing more to be done. We're a sitting duck now. Sound abandon ship and get in the boats, quick as you can. They'll probably be putting a couple of shots into us to keep us quiet, so keep your heads down. Good luck."

The bridge emptied rapidly as we followed the skipper's orders. The one thing I heard, though, as we were evacuating, and which has stayed with me to this day, was the song that was playing on the radio. It was a very popular tune at the time, "Begin the Beguine", but ever since then I have been unable to listen to it, as it will always be, for me, associated with ill-fortune and losing a good ship. By the time I reached the main deck most of the lifeboats had been launched, and I could already see several of them pulling clear of the ship. I found myself working with the chief and a couple of others to get the last boat lowered before taking hold of one of the ropes to slide down to it once it was in the water. I paused, though, before I left the deck for the last time, and had one last look around at the ship which had been my home for so many months. When you work on a ship for any length of time it becomes as easy and familiar to you as any home on land, with an emotional attachment far more than might be imagined for a floating hunk of iron. There were now only two of us left on board, the chief engineer Cecil Hutton and myself.

All of a sudden a massive detonation occurred just behind the bridge, and snapped me sharply out of my reverie. The raider had sent a shell slamming into the wallowing ship, and now as my eyes followed a line back to the enemy vessel I could see that they had launched a boat themselves, obviously with a boarding party on board. As it later transpired the radio operator on the German vessel had reported to his captain that the *Benarty* was still transmitting warning messages, and this had prompted them to open fire once again, when in reality he had simply picked up another ship re-transmitting our original warning.

"C'mon son, time to get going." The chief laid a hand on my shoulder as he ushered me over the side in front of him, and it was with a sense of unreality that I let myself slide down the rope and into the lifeboat. We pushed ourselves off from the hull with the oars, and then bent our backs into putting as much distance between the now-burning merchantman and ourselves. The fact that our ship was doomed was bad enough, but to all our minds now came the thought that our own fates were far from certain. By this stage of the war just about everybody who worked in the merchant marine had lost friends and relatives and had also heard alarming stories of how the Germans dealt with prisoners of war, of sailors being machine-gunned in the water or run down and left to drown. We wondered if we were about to suffer a similar fate.

The German launch now approached one of the lifeboats and took onboard the skipper and a couple of the ship's officers, then headed for the *Benarty*. I watched as they came alongside the ship and scaled the superstructure, then saw them scurrying to and fro along the deck, silhouetted against the glow of a small fire burning cheerily behind the bridge. At this point my attention came back once more to our own predicament in the lifeboat, as I noticed the chief was guiding us ever closer to the raider herself. Eventually we found ourselves next to the looming hull, and nets were thrown down for us to climb aboard. Whilst standing in the boat before commencing my climb I estimated that she was bigger than the *Benarty*, but couldn't see any identifying marks on the hull. Slowly and reluctantly I commenced my climb to captivity, whilst unknown faces peered down at me from the deck of our conqueror.

We were the last of the lifeboats to arrive at the raider, and as we stepped onto the deck we were ushered aft to join our shipmates, lined up against the rail. There were nineteen of us there on deck, with the skipper, chief engineer and steward still aboard the *Benarty*, no doubt being made to help the German boarding party. Our Chinese contingent was taken straight below as soon as they were aboard. We were a pretty sorry-looking bunch assembled there, two or three of the men injured and all apprehensive about our prospects. A couple of Germans were left to guard us, brandishing rifles and shouting out commands in their native guttural to anybody who stepped out of line or turned to speak to their neighbours. All we could do was look back to our old ship, on which the fire now appeared to be under control, and wonder about the frenzied activity taking place on her decks. We could see various items of all shapes and sizes being flung or lowered carefully to the motor launch bobbing alongside, and after approximately half an hour the Germans seem to have satisfied themselves that they had gathered everything of value that could be carried. They then returned to their launch and set off back to rejoin their comrades. As we leaned over the side we saw them arrive and begin to offload just about everything that had not been nailed down on the *Benarty*: food, clothes, mail sacks, radios, clocks and tools were all carried up the gangway to the deck, and two of the lifeboats were hauled aboard and stowed away, whilst the rest were smashed up and sunk. Even the nice little dinghy that we kept on board was brought onto the raider; over the ensuing weeks it was stripped down to the bare wood by their crew and carefully restored and re-varnished. We found out later that the German captain was an enthusiastic yachtsman who had spent a lot of time sailing the lakes and coastline of England, and who intended to transport our dinghy back to Germany for his own personal use.

We were cheered by the sight of Captain Watt and our two other shipmates being led down the deck to join us, and the guards were feeling relaxed and confident enough by this time to allow him to address us and inform us of what had been taking place on the *Benarty*.

"When the Jerries took us back on board they thought we might have booby-trapped her, so they kindly invited us to go first", the skipper explained.

"They had a look in the holds to see what we were carrying, then went back to the bridge and the living quarters and ransacked the place. They've brought all the clothes and food they could find, as I think they're running short on supplies, and I also believe that there are a lot of other British prisoners aboard.

"Boys, we're now prisoners of war aboard a German raider. They've promised me that we'll be well-treated as long as we're not too uncooperative, and we'll only be kept on board until they find a friendly port to off-load us at. The most worrying thing they told me is that they're currently being hunted by our navy because of their previous successes, and the chances are that if they get caught the navy boys won't stop to ask if any of their countrymen are aboard before they blow her out of the water!"

This was something I hadn't yet considered, and it certainly didn't cheer me up at all.

"Once they'd got everything down to the boat they went back and laid three timed charges, forward, aft and midships. She's got about five minutes, boys, so take a good last look if you want."

At that we all turned to look at the old ship in silence, each of us deep in our own thoughts. Before five minutes had passed, I believe, the first of the charges went off, followed in quick succession by the other two. Her stern lifted well clear of the water with the final detonation, and then began to quickly settle as sea water rushed in through the gaping holes the explosions had made. She remained side-on to us as her prow began to lift to heaven, steam exploding from her funnel as the cold water reached her boilers, and she creaked and groaned as rivets burst and plates twisted. As she came to the vertical she let out one more rush of steam before rapidly accelerating backwards towards the depths. Finally only her prow remained visible, but very quickly this too disappeared beneath the all-engulfing waves, as the *Benarty* started its mile-long journey to the bottom of the ocean, out of the sight of men.

BORN A BEACHCOMBER

Chapter Five

We were now prisoners on one of the infamous "ghost ships". These were a fleet of eleven heavily-armed auxiliary cruisers that were disguised as merchant ships, who between them, in their warfare from the shadows, did greater damage to the allied cause than the more famous German capital ships like *Bismarck* or *Tirpitz*. Our particular raider was able to present a total of twenty-six different silhouettes to an observer, had a dummy funnel as well as removable masts, flags from every sea-faring nation and the crew would dress in various costumes including women's clothing in order to present an innocent face to the world. Her armament, apart from the Heinkel HE-114B seaplane that had strafed us and the six 150mm guns that had been brought to bear on us earlier, included one 75mm gun on the bow, two twin 37mm anti-aircraft guns, four 20mm automatic cannon and four torpedo tubes. She could also lay mines and carried a total of ninety-two of these. Flaps in the side had been lowered to allow four of the 150mm guns to fire on us, the others being concealed in a fake crane construction. We were her eighth victim out of the twenty-two she would eventually sink or capture.

Once the Germans had stowed away the goods they had removed from our ship, they turned their attention to us. An officer approached us, introduced himself to the skipper then addressed the whole group:

"You are on board the cruiser *Atlantis*; you are all now prisoners of war. If you behave well you will be treated well, but any behaviour contrary to the good running of this ship will not be tolerated. The doctor will inspect you now."

With this we were formed into a queue, and waited our turn to be examined by the medical officer. Johnny Cogle and two of the other boys who were injured had their wounds dressed properly, while the rest of us were given a clean bill of health. The doctor was none too impressed when he looked at my teeth though, and in fact I had been getting pain from a couple of them for several weeks now, but I said nothing and he passed on to the next man. As the doctor completed his examination two officers strolled down the deck toward us, and from his cap insignia we realised that one of them was the captain. They stopped in front of us, looked us over, and the German captain turned to his colleague and made a remark, at which the other chuckled to himself, before they began moving on down the deck. At that point I said to the man standing next to me, "I wonder what he just said about us that was so funny?"

The captain's companion obviously overheard my question, turned back to me and said, "Captain Rogge said that you are undoubtedly a beachcomber!" before turning away and resuming his conversation.

I wasn't certain what being called a beachcomber signified to a German, though I was pretty sure it wasn't a compliment, but it was certainly a fairly accurate description of how I had spent a good deal of my time before leaving home, so I wasn't inclined to take offence. After this one of the Germans led us down below to our new quarters, which we found were already almost fully occupied by crewmen from ships attacked by the *Atlantis* before she found us. Despite the crowded surroundings the lads already there shifted themselves around and made space for us so that we all managed to get a bunk to ourselves for the time being, these being arranged in triple-tier. Our new home was on the lowest level of the *Atlantis*, and the heat, the smell of body-odours mixed with the smell of diesel, the constant hum and throb of the engines all made for uncomfortable lodgings. Within ten minutes, though, despite the discomfort, I fell into a deep sleep as all the nervous tension of the past few hours caught up with me. The adrenaline that had been running through my body since we had first sighted the raider had taken its toll, and though it had masked my exhaustion up until now, unconsciousness swept over me and I slept a dreamless sleep for the next six hours solid.

Over the next ten days we fell in with the rhythm of the enemy ship as we adapted to the fact that we were no longer free men. This is painful for anyone to accept, but for us free-spirited ocean travellers it is a particularly hard pill to swallow. We found, though, that our captors did nothing to make our captivity any harder than it already was, and indeed did their best to treat us reasonably. The quarters were unavoidably cramped, and food was not in abundance, but we did receive three meals a day and were given an allowance of ten pence daily, which enabled us to purchase some small

Two appearances of German raider Atlantis. *The ship could disguise itself in various ways, including raising a second, dummy, funnel (above), telescopic masts, wooden guns, even down to the details of women's clothing for the crew for the pretence of being a passenger ship.*

essentials such as toothpaste and soap from the stores, and enjoy a beer or a dram of scotch from the canteen. The German crew had pilfered everything they could carry from our old ship, and had taken all our personal valuables from us, including a watch given me by my father. In return, though, the shipboard routine was fairly leisurely considering we were prisoners of war, and we were allowed on deck for fresh air and exercise for three hours each morning and afternoon. It so happened that for several days after our capture the weather was set fair, and a hazy white sun beat down on us from a flawless blue sky, warming our faces and our spirits during our deck-side excursions. At night, though, some of the men became quiet, sullen even, as soon as we were locked in for the night and heard the hatches being bolted shut. We knew that they were locking us in to what was potentially our coffin, as if the *Atlantis* ran into a British warship then our countrymen would shoot first and worry about who had been on board once we were heading to the bottom. Some men would counter this air of foreboding by being overly talkative, but most of us just carried on with whatever we had to occupy our time and tried not to be too concerned with matters over which we had no control.

After five days my toothache had worsened to the point where I was willing to ask for help from the Germans. I approached the duty officer, and he arranged for me to see the ship's dentist. He was a thickset man with a grip like a vice, and once he had yanked my jaw open and spied the offending molars I knew I was in for it. He tut-tutted and shook his head;

"You know, you people never look after your teeth. Eat sweets all day, no cleaning at night. So don't complain to me if this hurts!"

With that he took up his pliers and almost before I knew what was happening I was looking down at three blackened teeth lying in a bowl in front of me. As it turned out he knew his trade well, and took the teeth out so skilfully that I had hardly felt a thing. The relief I felt was immediate, and I remember musing on the fact that I had had to wait until I had been captured by the Germans to experience my first visit to the dentist. At home seeing a dentist could be a costly experience, and we had never had the money for it. When I got back to the bunkroom I told Johnny and the rest of the boys about the treatment. Andrew Sandison now decided he would see what the dentist could do for him, eventually having several fillings that he was more than pleased with, and for the next few days the dentist found himself with a steady stream of British patients in various stages of dental disrepair knocking on his door.

On the tenth night in captivity our apprehension grew as we were woken by the engines increasing their revolutions. The ship began to pitch and roll more violently as the speed increased, and the bunks shuddered with the vibrations as she leapt forward at full speed ahead. Most of us were now awake and had quickly dressed ourselves, sitting nervously in the dark on the edge of our bunks, smoking in quick, shallow draws and looking around edgily in the miniscule glow of the tips of the cigarettes, wondering what would come next. The ship made rapid headway for approximately an hour, before the engines slowed to an idling speed. We could now hear the loud slap of the waves against the side of the hull as she sat virtually still in the water, but all at once this was drowned out as guns roared in the darkness.

"It's the bloody navy – trust 'em to turn up just when you don't want 'em!" one of my fellow captives muttered as the rest of us held a collective breath.

No impact was felt or heard aboard the raider, and the guns swiftly fell silent. Sweat was running down the back of my neck, and the tension was palpable.

"That was just our guns firing," somebody else ventured in the gloom, "she must have found another merchantman."

At this the guns started up once more, and this time I counted about fifty shots fired before silence returned. There was no doubt now, as the *Atlantis* had fired off such a high number of shells and received none in return, that she must have indeed run down another poor unfortunate like ourselves, and had just pounded them into submission, if not sunk them. We all felt sorry for the ship on the receiving end of the firing, but I can't deny that I was mightily relieved that our initial fears were unfounded, and that our own countrymen were not unknowingly sending us to the black depths below – for one more night, at least.

For a time we could hear activity of some kind going on outside our prison, including the distinct sound of a boat being lowered. After another hour voices could be heard in the corridor outside, followed by the door being unlocked and the lights turned on. We all peered, blinking in the harsh electric light, at the bedraggled, bewildered bodies now filing in to join our captivity. Ten days prior that had been me, but now mine was one of the comforting pair of hands reaching out to help the new POW's find somewhere to slump down in exhaustion, inwardly cursing their luck at falling prey to this lone raider but grateful for their own survival through such a bombardment. They were from a requisitioned French passenger ship, the *Commissaire Ramel*, which had been carrying a mixed cargo from Australia to England. Sixty-three survivors came aboard, mostly English but also a number of French and a Scottish skipper, and our living quarters were now full to bursting.

The latest arrivals took the number of prisoners on board the *Atlantis* to close on three hundred. We were crammed together like the proverbial sardines, and it's not surprising to note that though we all tried to get along there were times when tempers became frayed. We were something of a league of nations, with faces of every hue and voices chattering in every language and dialect. We had men from all four corners of the United Kingdom, from Shetland to Cornwall and from Essex to Anglesey. There were men from the colonies: Australia, New Zealand, Canada and India, along with French, Portuguese, Norwegians, Swedes, Africans and Arabs. The only contingent missing were the Chinese, who had not been confined with the rest of us. The ship's doctor had diagnosed some illness amongst them once they had come aboard, and he had placed them in quarantine for several days. Once he was satisfied there was no contagion they were released and quartered with the ship's own Asiatic crew, and put to work in the kitchens and laundry and as stewards. The German crew were mostly of a friendly disposition, and would exchange greetings in English whenever our paths crossed on deck, though from what I could gather they were none too pleased at the length of time they had been away from home, and were anxious about the progress of the war. They were also unhappy about the drop in their rations, as with so many mouths to feed, the captain had had to take drastic measures to ensure their supplies lasted. It was obvious that Captain Rogge would have to take some action to reduce the number of prisoners he was holding, for the sake of both the physical and mental well-being of all aboard, and that he would have to do it soon.

After sinking the *Commissaire Ramel* the *Atlantis* appeared to be sailing in an approximately eastward direction, obviously seeking further victims whilst hoping to avoid any contact with British warships. Time passed slowly for crew and prisoners alike, and not even a distant smokestack was spotted for the next month. If the weather was good we would spend our deck-time dozing in the sun, eyelids heavy, in that trance-like state somewhere between sleep and consciousness. If it was wet we would exercise in the rain, before returning, sodden but refreshed, to our troglodytic existence. Conditions below were uncomfortable but certainly not intolerable. The food was basic; bread, dried meat or an occasional stew, potatoes but rarely any other vegetable, though we did get an apple now and again. Our water ration was a quart a day which was barely enough in the heat of the Indian Ocean, and our discomfort was further exacerbated by the sweltering humidity down in the bowels of the ship. Our prison had not been designed for three hundred men, and although the bunks were stacked three-high there were still men stretched out on every inch of floor space. Sanitary facilities were remarkably good, with just enough toilets and wash basins to go around, and we worked hard to keep them clean and disinfected. As men who are thrown together in these circumstances will do, we grumbled amongst ourselves about our plight, and, although we knew we were lucky to be alive we still felt sorry for ourselves at times. Little did we know that our captivity at sea up to this point was something akin to a pleasure cruise compared with what was waiting ahead.

On the morning of 22nd October we were woken once more by the racing of the engines and an alarm being sounded throughout the ship. We knew from our time on deck and by making some rough calculations that the *Atlantis* was heading for the Sunda Strait, the channel between the islands of Java and Sumatra, and which links the Indian Ocean to the Java Sea. We also knew that she would be bound to find further victims in this area, due to it being a bottleneck which merchantmen had to enter and leave, although there was also an increased chance of the raider herself being intercepted, and this again increased our nerves. This time the pursuit didn't appear to have lasted long, as the engines quickly returned to an idling speed and there was no sound from the guns. No new prisoners appeared, and we were left wondering what was happening. Our guards were later than normal to let us out for an airing that morning, and as we trooped out topside we found the answer to our questions. An old tramp steamer was lying off our port bow, lying still in the water. She looked like she hadn't seen a dry-dock for several years, being covered in rust and in particular need of a lick of paint, and had obviously not been in any fit state to either fight or flee the German raider. This was the *Durmitor*, a Yugoslav ship of 5,623 tons, which had been in the process of carrying 8,200 tons of bulk salt from Torrevieja in Spain to Hiroshima in Japan. She had a crew of about forty men, and we were all wondering where these new prisoners were going to be squeezed in. This time there was to be no transfer of prisoners to the *Atlantis*, however; Captain Rogge had decided that the time had come to offload his captives and the newly captured ship would be ideal to transfer us to the African mainland.

I watched from the rails of the *Atlantis* as a dozen Germans were motored out to the *Durmitor*, which then made steam and disappeared over the horizon. The raider continued her patrol and we returned to our quarters but that evening Captain Rogge himself appeared before us with one of his officers who spoke excellent English, to inform us of his intentions. He told us that the *Durmitor* would be rendezvousing with us in four days, and that by then enough of the salt cargo would have been removed in order to allow room for the prisoners to be accommodated on top of it (we would be meeting about two hundred miles south of Christmas Island in fact, though he didn't give us that particular information at the time). He told us that it was not going to be a comfortable crossing and that food and water would be strictly rationed, but that it should only take two weeks to reach our destination. We were also warned against insurrection which would be dealt with in the most ruthless manner.

Once he had given us the news and left we got together to discuss the perceived pros and cons of our impending voyage. None of us liked the sound of the conditions on board, but this was countered by the fact that the Royal Navy would no longer be likely to sink us on sight. We figured that we could stick it out for two weeks and maybe it wouldn't be as bad as it sounded, and in any case we were all sick and tired of our current captivity, so at least it would be a change. However, the thirty days we eventually ended up being on board the *Durmitor*, more than double the intended time, later served to modify our opinions somewhat.

On the morning of 26th October the *Durmitor* once more hove into sight, and the Germans began transferring us across. The process took several hours due to the large number of prisoners, but as soon as we were out of the way and their own men back on board the raider started to make steam and head away. As she grew smaller in the distance I took a last look at the ghost-ship and hoped that she wouldn't find good hunting, wherever she was bound. The officers and crew had treated us fairly though, whilst on board, something that couldn't always be said for all merchant sailors captured in a similar way. I later heard from colleagues who had been taken on board the *Atlantis*'s sister ship, *Pinguin*, for instance, that her skipper ran a far harsher regime than that we experienced.

Atlantis would go on to be the second most successful of the raiders after *Pinguin*. Over the course of her six hundred and twenty-two day patrol, travelling over one hundred and two thousand miles in total, she sank or captured nearly 150,000 tons of allied shipping. Her own demise was not to come until late in 1941, and would result in another journey of epic proportions, this time undertaken by her own crew, who found themselves the hunted rather than the hunters, being hounded relentlessly on their quest to reach home.

In October 1941 she was given the task of re-supplying the U-boats operating in South African waters, rounding Cape Horn at the end of that month and entering the South Atlantic. On 22nd November she was to rendezvous with *U-126* 350 miles north-west of Ascension Island. As she was pumping oil across to the submarine, and while the U-boat skipper,

Lieutenant Bauer, was being treated to breakfast on-board *Atlantis*, the British cruiser *Devonshire* appeared over the horizon. The U-boat made an emergency dive, leaving its skipper on the raider, while the cruiser launched its Walrus seaplane to have a closer look at proceedings. The Germans had no time to haul in the hose-pipe being used in the re-fuelling, and the sight of this floating amidst a spreading slick of oil was an obvious clue to what had been happening, resulting in the seaplane signalling "s-s-s" back to the cruiser – submarine.

The raider attempted to put on the appearance of an innocent merchantman by transmitting their identity as the Greek ship *Polyphemus*, but the code they used was out of date, and before long the eight-inch guns of the cruiser were booming from ten miles distant, well out of range of the *Atlantis*'s weapons. Captain Rogge hoped the U-boat might attack the cruiser, but she had dived deeper when she heard the rumble of shells, and now had no idea what was happening on the surface. *Atlantis* was now being pounded despite making smoke to cover her tracks, and could not make much headway due to the port engine being put out of action. Rogge gave the order to abandon ship and set charges to scuttle the ship. They managed to launch their lifeboats before the charges went off, and, as the raider sank beneath the waves, the *Devonshire* retired from the engagement, not daring to stop to pick up survivors for fear of the U-boat in the vicinity.

As the survivors gathered together in the life-boats (only seven crewmen had been killed in the encounter) the U-boat re-surfaced, taking on board the wounded and allowing the captain the chance to take back his command. The U-boat then took six life-boats in tow for an intended journey of nearly a thousand miles to Brazil, though within a couple of days they had been overtaken by the German supply ship *Python*, a former liner, which took the crew onboard. *Python* had orders to carry on re-supplying U-boats in the vicinity and then ferry the *Atlantis* survivors back home. Rogge knew that they could not afford to relax, even though they appeared to have found an apparently comfortable salvation on board the ex-liner. Sure enough, on 1st December, whilst pumping oil to two U-boats in similar circumstances to how *Atlantis* had been surprised, a British cruiser appeared at a distance of nineteen miles. Once again the U-boats made immediate crash-dives, leaving the supply ship to its fate. *Python* tried to make a run for it but was soon overtaken by eight-inch shells crashing in the water all around, so the captain decided to bow to the inevitable and ordered "abandon ship".

The crew and survivors of the *Atlantis* scrambled to get into the lifeboats, while charges were set to send *Python* to the bottom, and once again the British cruiser, this time the *Dorsetshire*, left the scene once her prey was dispatched due to the suspected menace of U-boats in the vicinity. Now there were four hundred and fourteen men left floating in lifeboats, with over five thousand miles of hostile sea to cover before they could reach home waters. The two U-boats surfaced when they felt the danger had passed, taking some of the survivors on board and the little flotilla of eleven lifeboats and seven rubber dinghies in tow. They were later joined by two further U-boats, dividing the men up so that each submarine carried just over one hundred extra men and abandoning the lifeboats; in mid-December four Italian U-boats joined them at the Cape Verde Islands and took a share each of the survivors. They eventually reached St. Nazaire on Christmas Day, their entire voyage having totalled six hundred and fifty-five days and having been sunk themselves on two occasions.

A few weeks after we had been transferred to the *Durmitor*, the *Atlantis* made her most significant contribution to the war. On 11st November she chased down the Blue Funnel liner *Automedon*; firing from two thousand yards, a salvo of shells destroyed the bridge, killing the captain and all the officers on board. Their deaths prevented the destruction of secret papers that were being carried on the ship, and the subsequent boarding party from *Atlantis* found them intact. Part of this haul was secret mail addressed to the British Commander-in-Chief, Far East, including a comprehensive report on the defence plans for the Far East and Singapore, including details of the allied land, sea and air forces. The report was written in a pessimistic tone, the intimated conclusion being that Britain was not likely to emerge as the winner in a military conflict with the Japanese empire. It was eventually handed over to Japanese Naval Intelligence, and Admiral Yamomoto concluded from its contents that if he could knock America out of the war then the British Empire would not have the strength to resist alone. The captured information therefore had a significant role in leading to both the attack on Pearl Harbor in December 1941 and the fall of Singapore a couple of months later.

For this service to Japan Captain Rogge was awarded a Katana Samurai sword, one of only three awarded in the war to non-Japanese personnel, the other recipients being Goering and Rommel. Rogge would go on to become a vice-admiral in the German navy, and survived not only the war itself but also managed to avoid the war-crimes trials that so many of his fellow countrymen of similar rank were subjected to after 1945. This was entirely due to his often-reported reputation for good treatment of prisoners and strict adherence to the Geneva Convention rules concerning them. Although he was responsible for the deaths of many allied seamen during the course of his attacks on merchant shipping, he would never hesitate to pick up survivors, showing a humane concern for their welfare

Kapitan Bernhard Rogge, German raider Atlantis.

and never allowing his ship or crew to be associated with any atrocities. He not only survived with his honour intact, he positively thrived in the post-war period, culminating in being made a rear-admiral in the West German Bundesmarine in 1957, serving as part of the NATO alliance alongside many of his former adversaries.

As our launch approached the *Durmitor* I noted what a beautiful morning it was, with a placid sea and a cool breeze blowing through the balmy air. I had held on to my earlier optimism as we began the move, but I believe that most of us had our first feelings of apprehension as we neared the ship and saw up close what poor condition she was in. Her paintwork was badly flaked and missing altogether in places, and the hull and superstructure were rotten with rust. The deck was caked in salt, and bright green algae was taking a hold in every nook and cranny due to lack of washing down. Worse was to come though, as we were led to our accommodation. Just enough of the salt cargo had been cleared from no.1 and no.2 holds to allow men to be housed on top of the remainder, and over a hundred were packed into each one. We were given tarpaulins to spread over the salt, and that was the extent of our comforts. We had no blankets, pillows or bedding of any sort, and after the tarpaulins had been walked over a few times they became damp and filthy. The first day on board saw us trying to make ourselves as comfortable as possible, making pathetic attempts to smooth out a small area where we could each lie out and rest, but it soon became evident that our best efforts would be thwarted, as with each movement the salt beneath us would shift and lump up. As morning turned to noon the hold heated up and the salt began to sweat and stink, and it was then that I first noticed the cockroaches. Firstly they were scuttling to and fro around the edges of the hold, but soon enough they were everywhere and their legs would beat a tattoo on the tarpaulins as they skittered and crawled over and around us and got into everything.

We were given a small plate of boiled rice to eat that afternoon, then in the evening a small lump of black bread and a cup of tea. When we were allowed on deck we found that we were separated from the German crew on the bridge by thickly-laid coils of barbed wire. There was also a machine gun fixed on the bridge which covered all possible points of intrusion; as we gathered on the deck Lieutenant Dehnel, who was the officer in charge, let us know in no uncertain terms what would happen to any unwelcome visitors. He also gave us a demonstration by firing the machine gun into the sea and ordering two of his men to lob grenades over the side, just to remind us of the firepower at their disposal.

That night, as the hatches to the hold were banged shut and locked, I reflected on how foolishly simple my optimism had been that morning, and set about trying to iron myself an area flat enough to sleep on. As the evening wore on the temperature in the hold plummeted, and what had been a roasting oven during the day became little more than a refrigerator packed with shivering bodies at night. I tried to make myself as comfortable as possible and was drifting in and out of sleep when something pattered over my body and brought me fully awake and bolt upright. The hold was now beginning to ring with shouts and curses as others were woken or disturbed by small, dark, hairy bodies that scampered over and around them as they lay, bodies with a long, hairless tail at one end and sharp teeth and beady eyes that twinkled in the gloom at the other – rats, and lots of them.

After the first night, when even these unwelcome visitors and uncomfortable conditions had failed to stop us falling into an exhausted slumber, the hatches were unlocked and we were allowed out onto deck and given breakfast. This was a small lump of black bread about the size of a tennis ball and half a cup of water. Occasionally in the early days this was supplemented by a cup of tea and sometimes a few spoonfuls of porridge, but as the supplies dwindled so these luxuries disappeared. The rest of the day was spent doing very little, mostly seeking shade as the day warmed up; the exposed deck reflected and amplified the burning sunshine, while the hold quickly became airless and stifling. We were given nothing to eat or drink between breakfast and dinner, which appeared late in the afternoon. This consisted of either a small plate of rice or a bowl of watery bean soup, along with another half cup of water. This was our entire day's ration finished now, and we could expect nothing more until the next morning.

The Germans had reckoned on the *Durmitor* taking two weeks to make landfall in Axis-occupied East Africa, though they had only been able to spare one week's supply of bread. Food was therefore already in short supply from the outset, with water even more scarce, but this was compounded by the discovery of a large hollow space under the coal in the bunker. It was a common swindle to load a ship with a lot less coal than she'd paid for, and meant that there would not be fuel enough to reach the coast. Speed was reduced to conserve supplies, but this in turn extended the journey time. The food and drink ration, already inadequate, was cut further so as to be virtually non-existent. Our deteriorating conditions led many on board to start talking about taking over the ship, but although it made us feel better to talk about it, I don't believe that anyone really thought we had a chance of overpowering the well-armed Germans. This doubt became a certainty after a couple of weeks, when malnutrition began to work its effect on our bodies and minds; but worse than the lack of food was the thirst. For the first part of the journey there was no rain, only incessant, burning heat during the day followed by nights lying on salt that was in the very air you breathed, getting caked to the back of your throat and cracking the skin at the corners of your mouth. When the thirst became unbearable, a few of us decided that it would be worth breaking the night-time curfew and getting up to the deck, where it would at least be cooler, though we ran the risk of being shot if we were spotted. We managed to prise the hatches apart just enough to allow a thin man (by this time most of us) to squeeze through. Once on deck we had two priorities: firstly to find something to drink and secondly to avoid catching a bullet from a sentry. We would take any moisture we could find, whether it was the condensation on the pipe work or a drop or two of liquid from opening the taps on the winches – even if it only wet our lips and tasted of rust it was still precious to us.

By this time the crew had begun to strip the ship of any wooden fittings, cannibalising it in order to feed the furnaces and keep up a head of steam, which meant breaking up furniture, doors, derricks and even the hatch covers, making our night-time forays much easier. After two weeks of struggling on at three knots the monsoon broke, and the Germans decided to use the hatch-cover tarpaulins as sails, taking advantage of the swirling, powerful winds that stirred up the sea around us. We welcomed the rain as heaven-sent to begin with, and set to collecting it in anything that came to hand, slaking our thirst and laughing wildly just at the feeling of the heavy rain-drops hitting our faces. It soon became apparent that this change in the weather also brought with it some serious problems for us, though. The hatch-covers had been removed to burn for fuel, and the tarpaulins were now being hoisted as sails, leaving the holds exposed to the elements. The rain was beating straight onto the bulk salt, and our living and sleeping area was fast turning to quicksand. The wet salt got into everything and coated you as you slept, drying your skin out and making you susceptible to sores and ulcers, which would in turn attract the assorted vermin sharing your sleeping quarters.

After four weeks living like this a lot of the men were suffering badly from the combined effects of malnutrition, thirst and unsanitary living conditions, and many began falling sick. It was a real blessing, then, when we sighted land on 23rd November, after twenty-nine days at sea. This was the little village of Warsheik on the coast of Somaliland, and though the sight cheered us the ship had not quite finished with us yet. As we approached the shore our captors managed to run her aground on a sunken coral reef, and she stuck fast. After deciding that the ship was there for good the German lieutenant gave the order to break out the remaining lifeboat, and the arduous task of ferrying the prisoners ashore began. This process took several hours, and as I was one of the younger and fitter ones I was left as one of the last to disembark. As it happened I had to wait even longer than anticipated to make my trip in the lifeboat, as the tide turned and the *Durmitor* drifted off the reef of her own accord, causing more consternation as the anchor now had to be deployed. Eventually my turn came, ending my time as a prisoner at sea as I now stepped ashore to become a POW on African soil, in Italian Somaliland.

BORN A BEACHCOMBER

Chapter Six

Waiting to greet us on the ramshackle Warsheik jetty was a contingent of nervous-looking Italian soldiers, some of whom shouted at us in their own tongue and gestured with their raised rifles to point us in the direction of the assortment of huts which comprised the settlement. A crowd of Somalis had gathered to see what all the fuss was about when the Italian troops deployed to meet the arriving boats, and they now looked on impassively as we trudged along the road into town.

The Italians seated us in what had once been the parade square of a deserted barracks complex, where we found what shade we could from the burning African sun, and issued us each with a cup of water, but no food. They then posted sentries and for the most part seemed to lose interest in us, wandering off to find their own shelter from the sun and leaving us to lie around and sleep or sit and chat amongst ourselves. The guards weren't over-zealous about their duties, probably because we were obviously in no fit condition to present any kind of threat and escape was futile at this point, as where would we go? In fact I got the feeling that most of the troops would have welcomed us disappearing off into the bush as it would have meant good riddance to a responsibility they could well do without.

As the afternoon wore on the only person who appeared to take any notice of us at all was an attractive young white woman who appeared on the edge of the square, looked us over for a couple of minutes and promptly disappeared again. Half an hour or so later she re-appeared and to our surprise addressed us in a crisp, middle-English accent.

"I am led to believe that you men haven't eaten properly for some time, so my husband has given instructions that you are to be properly fed before you are transferred to the nearest POW camp."

Though the thought of being moved again was not one we relished, the promise of food was very welcome. Our guardian angel turned out to be the English wife of an Italian army major, and she was certainly easier on the eye than the food turned out to be on the stomach! Her husband had persuaded a local Italian farmer to slaughter two of his goats, and a handful of his native workers now appeared with the freshly butchered carcasses and a large cooking pot which they set up in the square, filled with water, set a fire and proceeded to chuck large slabs of meat into. Once our "chefs" considered the meat done we formed an orderly queue to receive a sliver or two of blanched, light-greenish flesh, which would definitely have benefited from the addition of roast potatoes, carrots, sprouts and gravy. There wasn't quite enough to go round, so the chefs threw the innards into the pot as well, leaving the men at the back of the queue to receive a plate of steaming offal. I only took a small plate of meat, as I didn't think my stomach would cope with digesting too much solid food after a month of virtual inactivity.

That night proved to me that I had been right to be cautious, as a good number of the men doubled up with stomach cramps, with most of them making a dash for the perimeter of the settlement, the hut which had been allocated as our bathroom being unable to cope with the demand. Despite the violent reaction of some of the men's constitutions to the food on offer we were still more than grateful for what the officer's wife had done for us, perhaps as much for being treated with a little human kindness as for the sustenance provided, and would have liked to have thanked her for her action. Unfortunately that was the last we ever saw of her.

Towards evening a couple of Italian soldiers appeared and unlocked the barracks halls, informing us in broken English that this is where we would spend the night, as transport which would take us to a more permanent camp would not be available until the following day. With that they made themselves scarce once more, while we found ourselves a patch of floor (the beds were long-gone) and those who weren't so badly affected by the earlier meal threw themselves down to sleep. I slept soundly that night, though I woke just before sunrise; I could still feel the motion of the boat in my head as I lay on the wooden floor, so I decided to have a walk along the coast before the heat became too intense later in the day. Nothing was stirring around the barracks, so I wandered out and through the village, heading for the seashore where I had noticed some native fishing boats pulled up when we were landing the day before. I was disappointed to find the boats gone, though whether they had gone out the night before or earlier in the morning I had no idea. My disappointment stemmed from a half-baked plan I had made the night before, to take one of the boats and make a run for freedom, though where I would go and how far I would get was questionable. As I walked the shoreline and this alien land stretched out before me, bathed in early morning light and yet full of mystery, the realisation that I was very far from home hit me and I suddenly felt a need to be back amongst my shipmates. Before I turned to walk back, though, I took a moment to look around me, hearing the waves and the cries of the birds, feeling the sand beneath my feet and the warm wind on my face, appreciating the fact that I was still alive and standing on this beach on the other side of the world from the sands of Burrafirth. Not long after I arrived back at the barracks eight large Italian army trucks arrived to transport us the thirty miles or so south to our POW camp at Mogadishu.

The trucks had arrived with their own complement of guards to make sure we behaved ourselves on the hour-long transfer, and these fellows were either a little more zealous than the Italian soldiers we had encountered thus far, or just eager to get back to their own surroundings. This led to the first thing that had made us laugh for a long time, as they began herding not only the POWs into the open-backed trucks but also the protesting German sailors and the Yugoslav crew of the *Durmitor*. A red-faced Lieutenant Dehnel and his men were disarmed and shooed in with the rest of us, a situation that the Germans certainly didn't see as humorous as they sat together as a nervous bunch in the back amongst their former captives.

It so happened that none of us were really in any fit state to start any trouble with our enemies at that point, and in any case the Italians posted a couple of armed guards in with us, so all the Germans had to contend with were some ironic jibes and a few meaningful stares. When we reached Mogadishu they had to put up with being paraded through the town with the rest of us by the triumphant Italians; seeing them sitting dejectedly at the back of the truck somehow brightened the mood for the rest of us, and we started waving back at the passing crowds.

Our entertainment came to an end when we reached Autogruppo barracks on the outskirts of the town, and a senior officer finally took notice of the lieutenant's continual griping and had him and his men released. He had had his feathers ruffled and had lost his arrogant strut the last time we ever saw him, hurrying off indignantly to board a truck to take him back to Warsheik, so we gave him a rousing cheer and a few catcalls to see him on his way. In fact, Lt. Dehnel and his men went straight back to the *Durmitor*, still aground, and managed to refloat her. They then sailed her down the coast to Kismaayo, a small port town, and from there managed to get passage on the supply ship *Tannenfels*, which had been impounded in neutral Somaliland when the war had started. The *Tannenfels* then made rendezvous with the *Atlantis* in February, reuniting Dehnel and his men with Captain Rogge once again.

The other reason our amusement came to an end was when we saw the condition of the camp we were to be living in. Apparently an Italian army unit had been based here until recently, and unlike the previous barracks they had at least left the beds. That was to prove the only plus point, as they had also left it in a state of squalor. The barrack rooms were not, in fact, proper buildings at all, but were of a shanty construction often seen huddled in their thousands around modern day African cities, utilising all sorts of construction materials such as packing crates, corrugated iron, mud bricks and anything else that could be found to plug a hole. The camp adjoined a local airfield and the troops had been moved out when it was deemed to be at high risk of air raids from the British, obviously making it an ideal spot for keeping POWs. With the soldiers gone but piles of rotting food supplies left behind, the rats and cockroaches had moved in, so we were back to living in conditions not unlike those aboard the *Durmitor*.

In other ways conditions in Mogadishu turned out to be even worse than aboard the old Yugoslav steamer, as food was just as scarce as it had been then, but now consisted of mealy maize, rice and, if we were lucky, some rotten camel meat. The maize was simply alive with maggots, while the rice was contaminated with weevils, and to start with we would try to fish the maggots and weevils out and either flick them away or line them up like soldiers around the edge of the plate. Once we had done this we found that there was so little sustenance left on the plate that it was simply not worth eating, so after a few days most of us simply spooned the lot into our mouths. There was no sanitation at all for us in the camp, no running water and no proper latrine, just an area where we could dig a hole and squat, which also provided all shapes and sizes of flies and mosquitoes with a perfect breeding ground.

It was not surprising, then, that by as soon as the second day some of the men started going down with dysentery, and within days half the men in camp were suffering from this very unpleasant condition. My pal Gilbert was one of those more severely affected and was carted off to the local hospital where he laid with agonizing stomach cramps, his condition deteriorating for the next two weeks. To my amazement I seemed immune to whatever was laying the rest of the men low, and in all the camp I found only two other men who were similarly unaffected. One day I was allowed out to visit Gibby in the hospital, and I soon realised that they had virtually no chance of recovery there as conditions were just as unsanitary as in the camp. When I got back I made representations to one of the officers on duty, pleading with him to at least get the hospital cleaned up even if they wouldn't do anything about the camp. Although he spoke good English he simply pouted and shrugged his shoulders, so I was sure that I had made no impression on him but, for whatever reason, within a week a squad of Italian nurses were drafted into the hospital, setting to with mops, buckets and some long-overdue attention for their patients, and within another week the men were showing signs of recovery.

Gibby was one of those who made a full recovery, to my relief, although he had lost over five stones in weight; others weren't so lucky, and out of over ninety men hospitalised four had died and more would succumb over the following months and years from dysentery-related complications.

Christmas came and went with little cause for celebration in Mogadishu, as we were in the middle of the dysentery outbreak, and then New Year. By early 1941 most of the men were on the mend, and the Italian authorities decided that rather than clean up the Mogadishu camp it would be easier to transfer the prisoners. We found ourselves being loaded up and moved on again, this time to Merca, seventy miles to the south-west.

Arriving at Merca was literally a breath of fresh air, as the camp was situated less than a hundred yards from a beautiful golden beach that stretched as far as the eye could see in both directions, and the sea breezes were a more than welcome change from the constant stench of rotting and decay that we had lived with at Mogadishu. The huts were better built too, having previously stored bananas before the fruit was picked up and shipped off to Europe in happier and more prosperous times. In fact we found that the Italians were still storing various items in the huts when we arrived, so we were informed that our accommodation would not be ready for us until the following day. We were a pretty ragged bunch by this time, but the officer in charge also promised us some new clothes. Unfortunately the chef from Mogadishu appeared to have followed us to Merca, as we were served the usual rice and weevil special and a cup of weak tea, so some things had obviously not changed for the better. I found myself a clean, sandy spot on the ground near the wire fence of the compound and lay down with my hands behind my head, staring up at the hazy, blue sky, happy to feel the warm breeze and smell the ocean again.

As the sun dipped towards the horizon I fell into a deep slumber, and here began an intriguing episode for me that seems to be beyond rational explanation. As my eyes closed I began to dream, seeing a figure approaching me from a long distance away, slowly getting nearer and nearer until I recognised her as Helen Gray, an old lady in her seventies who was a friend of my mother's back in Unst. She seemed to be trying to talk to me but I couldn't quite hear what she was saying, just catching the odd snatch of sound that made no sense. I tried to tell her to shout but she was obviously having similar problems hearing me. She then faded from view and I woke with a start, the dream still fresh in my mind, thinking to myself how strange that I should dream of an old lady who I had neither seen nor thought of since I had left home. I thought no more of it until many months later, by which time I had finally arrived home. My family were relieved that I was safe and back with them once again, but my brother Jimmy was much more interested in dragging me outside and showing me what a Messerschmitt 109 had done to the gable end of the house when it had strafed all the croft-houses around Burrafirth than he was hearing about my misadventures. The damage was minimal thankfully, as the house was built of solid stone and was over three feet thick at that end, and no-one had been injured.

"I suppose everybody was worried about me, though, when the ship went missing and nobody knew if the crew got off or not?" I asked him.

"We were, but Helen Gray came over to see us early in the New Year and told Mother that there was nothing to worry about, as she kent you were safe and well."

"And just how did she know that?"

"No idea. But Mother just said Helen has always kent things that other people don't."

The old lady had turned up at Buddabrake at ten o'clock at night, with snow on the ground and a bitter easterly wind blowing in from the Siberian steppes. She had walked over three miles from her home, which was not an easy journey for a woman of her age and her state of health, but she had felt compelled to impart the information that had come to her that night. She was well known locally for having "second sight", which the local children always took to mean that she was a witch, but certainly no-one at the time, outside of our POW camp, knew we were alive. Our shipping company, William Thomson's of Leith, only knew that the *Benarty* was overdue, presumed lost to enemy action, and the first time we could get in touch with the outside world was after we were liberated at the end of February.

The other thing that puzzled me on waking up that first morning in the Merca camp was the addition of three puncture wounds on my left arm.

Two were close and parallel to each other, the third a little further up the arm. I hadn't felt a thing during the night, and had no pain on waking and no inflammation or swelling. One of the boys thought that a scorpion had stung me, as there were plenty around, but a little later on I was chatting with one of the African workers and he said that I'd been bitten by a bat. Apparently they carry some kind of anaesthetic in their saliva, and you wouldn't even know you'd been bitten if you didn't notice the wounds. Luckily I didn't suffer from any lasting ill-effects, though I also learnt that they sometimes transmit rabies, so was pleased to find that my bat was more hygienic than most.

Although conditions were generally better now the promised new clothes never turned up. We were all wearing rags by this time, so when somebody suggested a kick-around and asked if anybody would donate any spare material to make a football (of sorts) there were plenty of volunteers. We packed the rags together and bound them tightly with some old string that had once tied packages of bananas, ending up with a vaguely football-shaped affair that, though it would never grace Wembley, nevertheless provided us with a couple of hours amusement each day. I should say that it was pure amusement to start with, though the game started to take on an importance of its own after a while, as these things often do when there is very little else to distract you, so that after a week or so the competition became fierce. On one of these occasions one of the boys took an over-zealous kick at the ball and managed to punt it right over the fence and a good hundred feet or so beyond. The guard patrolling along the outside of the perimeter fence was a Somali, a local man, and one who took his duties very seriously. He studiously ignored our shouts and gesticulations to throw the ball back and carried on marching up and down outside the wire. Pat, a small but feisty Irishman, had enough of this after a couple of minutes.

"A couple of you boys hold the wire apart and I'll go and get the ball myself."

So I pulled on one side while one of the other players pulled on the other, and Pat slipped through the gap. He scampered over to the ball and collected it before turning back for the compound, but unfortunately the guard turned at this point and saw him. His first reaction was to reach for his rifle, which he unslung from his shoulder and tried to load a round into the chamber. Luckily for Pat the guard either had no idea what he was doing or the mechanism was jammed, and when he failed to get it working he rushed over to where Pat was just coming back in through the fence and started jabbing him with the barrel.

"Don't you poke me with that old thing" said Pat as he grabbed the rifle on our side of the fence and started a tug of war with the guard.

At just the right moment he let go and the Somali went sprawling on his back. We gave him a good cheer at that, which must have woken up the sentry's comrades in the guardhouse who came rushing out to his aid. Another of them tried loading the gun but to no avail, so they got another ironic cheer before we scarpered for the huts, just in case one of them remembered what he was supposed to be doing.

The camp at Merca held many different nationalities but for the most part we all got along well, most of us not having the strength to either give or take offence. The only trouble that did happen was an argument between two crewmen from a French merchantman, the older man accusing the younger one of being a fifth columnist and a spy for the Germans. He was convinced that their route had been betrayed to German agents before they had left port, and it seemed that most of his shipmates agreed with him. The heated words were obviously building up to a fight, and though I couldn't understand what they were saying the old man was making his intentions perfectly obvious, and a crowd started gathering around them. With just about the entire camp now encircling the two men, the camp commandant Captain Bracco and half a dozen of his guards made their way into the crowd, the captain ending up standing behind the suspected fifth columnist and listening to the haranguing he was receiving from the older man. Bracco was a sturdily built man himself, and always very smartly attired in well-pressed uniform, gold-braided hat and chest full of medals. Unfortunately for him he obviously didn't possess the quickest of reactions; when the older Frenchman decided that it was time for action rather than words and swung a giant haymaker at his adversary the latter ducked smartly out of the way, leaving Bracco to take the full force of the blow flush on the chin. We all roared our approval as he was propelled backwards, his medals rattling and his hat flying off in the opposite direction, to land in a crumpled heap in the dirt. Still stunned, he managed to stagger groggily to his feet and blow his whistle, at which a couple of his guards appeared, both Somalis trying and failing to suppress wide grins. They then marched the old Frenchman away to solitary confinement, accompanied by the cheers of the entire camp, while Bracco retrieved his hat, made a half-hearted attempt to straighten his uniform and made his way back to the guardhouse with far less dignity than he had had on the way out. As it turned out the Frenchman was to spend less than two weeks in solitary: our liberators were already heading for Merca with the Italian army putting up only a token resistance.

From 20th February onwards we began to notice a marked change in the behaviour of our captors, and a new tension filled the air. Of course we were told nothing, but all of a sudden the guards were no longer patrolling the perimeter fence but were employed emptying the possessions out of the Italian soldiers' quarters and starting mysterious fires behind the administration hut. A couple of days later a number of trucks appeared at the camp, and we all started speculating that we were about to be moved on to yet another camp, though hopefully not back to Mogadishu. We realised that the trucks were not for us when they were loaded with all the goods that had previously been emptied from our captors' huts and proceeded to roll out of camp at speed, never to be seen again. We were still fed and watered as usual up to the night of the 24th February, when there was an even bigger commotion than previously, with the sound of engines running and vehicles departing, though we were unable to see anything in the dark African night. The next morning the camp was very quiet, with no movement of any kind happening outside the wire, and we were even more puzzled when no-one arrived to serve us our rice and weevils. Most of us believed that there was simply to be a changing of the guard, and the fact that one set of guards had packed up and gone before the relieving troop had arrived didn't surprise us, as that would simply be the Italian army operating to its usual perceived level of efficiency.

As the morning wore on I sat chatting with Gibby and Johnny and a few of the other *Benarty* boys, discussing the rapid exit of the camp guards and when we were likely to be fed next. When the sun had baked the ground where we were sitting to the point of discomfort we got up and strolled around the perimeter. Through the stifling heat a nice, fresh breeze was coming in off the sea, and all at once I noticed something else: there was a distant humming and a feeling almost as if the air around us was vibrating. The other boys now picked up on the sound too, and before long the entire camp was gathered at the southern fence, as the noise and vibration was definitely coming from somewhere south of us. It was getting louder and more distinct now, the sound of heavy motors mixed with a metallic grinding and clanking.

"Tanks," we muttered to ourselves and our neighbours, and there, appearing out of the heat haze to the south, came the unmistakable silhouettes of the mechanical juggernauts. For a few minutes the camp was in silence as a moving horde of vehicles, both tanks and trucks, solidified through the haze heading directly for us. In time of war a tank coming straight at you is an unnerving sight and we were more than a little perturbed by this turn of events – these were obviously not mere camp guards. Then, as I watched intently, something else appeared in the shimmering light, seeming to hover above the oncoming mass of machinery: colours started becoming visible, and suddenly there were the unmistakable red, white and blue of the Union Jack fluttering proudly at the head of the column.

"It's our lot!" someone shouted, and the biggest cheer yet heard in the camp erupted from several hundred parched throats.

We hadn't known it but the East Africa Corps had been working their way steadily along the coast, sweeping the hapless Italians ahead of them in full flight, and now they had reached the edge of what had been Captain Bracco's little domain. He had had the stomach, but not one for a fight, and had cleared out as soon as he heard the British were in the vicinity. We all stood back from the area around the gates as one of the tanks approached at speed, and without hesitating smashed them to the ground beneath his treads. This was met with another roar of approval, and as he came to a halt and vaulted down from his turret the tank commander suddenly found himself besieged by as pathetic and ragged a mob as he could have found anywhere in Africa, overcome with gratitude for their liberation.

More tanks and trucks were entering the compound now, troops disembarking and handing out cigarettes to the emaciated inmates. I took a long draw on the first decent tobacco I had tasted in a long time, sat down next to the fence and took a good look around. I wanted to remember this moment for a long time to come, 12.45pm on 25th February, the time I was given my freedom back, hoping that this would be the one and only time that it was taken from me. A mobile kitchen was now being set up at the rear of one of the trucks and already an orderly queue was being formed snaking towards it, so as soon as I had finished my smoke I jumped up and attached myself to the rear. When the grub had been prepared and served up I thought it tasted as good as anything to be found in the very best of restaurants, although it was only standard army fare, mutton stew with a few vegetables added. It was just such a luxury to be eating without half the meal staring back at you and trying to wriggle off the side of the plate.

The officer in charge addressed us after we had eaten, informing us that he had assigned trucks to take us on south to Mombasa, and that they would be setting out pretty much immediately. He apologised for not giving us time to bathe in the guards' quarters, but he had at least liberated a large number of brand new Italian army uniforms which we were to wear for the journey. They might be enemy uniforms but at least they were clean, so we tore off the remnants of the rags we were wearing and dressed ourselves up as El Duce's finest. It certainly felt a little odd to be dressed like this as we loaded into the trucks, drove out of the camp and pulled onto the road south – we just hoped that any passing Hurricane wouldn't mistake us for an enemy raiding party.

That evening the trucks came to a halt in what appeared to be a volcanic depression, forming a natural amphitheatre with high-sided cliff walls all around. As we ate the sun started to sink below the rim of the crater to the west, flooding the whole depression with a vivid pink light, the final rays of the sun glinting off the water of a small lake that sat at its very centre, and giving the whole place an air of magic. We had our evening rations and were then issued with a blanket roll each and told to find somewhere to bed down. Some of the boys stayed in and around the lorries, maybe being scared to stray too far from the symbols of their new-found freedom. Johnny, Gibby and I found a clearing about a hundred yards away where we lay talking about our liberation and the likelihood of getting home in the not-too-distant future. As the conversation died out I lay once more with my hands behind my head, listening to the sounds of the African night as the predators came out and the daytime shift retired, and staring up at a sky that was now blanketed with stars, far closer than they seemed to be at home, almost close enough to touch. That night I slept the deep, undisturbed sleep of a free man once again.

Thomas Mathieson's discharge papers.

BORN A BEACHCOMBER

Chapter Seven

Our journey south began with five days on rutted, bumpy tracks, during which we had a glimpse of the incredible African landscape and often received warm hospitality in villages where people appeared to have little or nothing of their own in the first place. The road mainly hugged the coast but was sometimes forced to loop inland for a distance to avoid a natural obstacle or follow a feature such as a dry watercourse.

We started out from Merca in an arid wilderness, but as we rolled on, normally covering less than a hundred miles in a day, the landscape evolved and became noticeably more verdant the further south we struck. The sun still beat down on us mercilessly, but sudden downpours now punctuated the trip, which were violent in their intensity but welcome nonetheless. As we got nearer to our destination the roads became progressively worse, deeply rutted with the continual cycle of rain turning them to mud followed by a baking sun. It was while we were making good time on one of these tracks that we happened to hit a particularly deep rut which sent all of us in the back into freefall; most of us simply ended up in a heap on top of each other, but my long-time travelling companion Gibby was not so lucky. He came down from a great height onto the tailboard of the truck, crying out in agony as his spine took the full force of landing, and spent the rest of the trip in constant pain which was only relieved slightly once he received drugs from the medical officer in Mombasa. He would be on medication for the rest of his life for a condition that was to be a constant reminder of his time in captivity and which severely limited his physical activity from that time on.

On the fifth day it was decided that the roads south were now impassable so we were re-directed to a small port on the coast where a cruiser waited to take us off. We had hoped that she would take us home, but in fact she was just filling in the rest of the journey to Mombasa, where she dropped us at a transit camp the next day. None of us were overly enamoured with the Royal Navy at this time, as we had all been wondering where they had been while the raider had been taking his fill in the Indian Ocean; despite numerous distress calls and many sinking's they never seemed to show up. We were even less happy the next day, as we were informed in the shipping office by a naval official, a weasly little man in an oversized cap, that we would have to work our passage home, there being a number of ships in port locally that required crewing. They would not even be heading straight back to Britain, but would mostly be re-crossing the Indian Ocean to take on another cargo. The official made it clear that he considered it our duty to comply with his wishes, and added "You are within your rights to refuse to cooperate, but non-compliance will result in the ceasing of payment of all dependants' allowances".

Weakened though I was, I had been in half a mind to do as he asked, if it would help the war effort. At this last threat, though, I had had enough, and, along with all the others, refused outright. We had been through too much lately to give in to this pompous official who I thought would have made a great right-hand man to our former camp commandant Bracco.

"In that case I will bid you good day, *gentlemen*, but I wouldn't get your hopes up of getting out of Mombasa anytime soon."

Due to our insistence that we were in no fit state to go back to work immediately, the British authorities in Mombasa obviously decided to file us away in a draw marked "non-urgent", and ensured that the wheels of bureaucracy turned ever-so-slowly as regards our repatriation. The transit camp was little better than the POW camp at Merca although the food contained a little more sustenance. We were now officially free men and could wander around the town as we chose, but lack of money meant that eating, drinking or any other distractions to break the monotony were not possible outside the perimeter of the camp. The local beaches were spectacular, however, and two or three of us would explore the coastline most days, trekking in the shade of the abundant vegetation bordering the sand during the worst heat of the day. We got chatting with some of the local fishermen one morning, and after I had demonstrated a few simple knots and how to splice a rope to them they invited me out fishing. I must admit that on first inspection their boat didn't appear overly robust or even seaworthy, but I thought "What the hell!" and clambered aboard. They were simple people but very enthusiastic and friendly, and I think they noticed that (as soon as I was satisfied it wasn't going to sink) I was quite at home in a small craft on the open ocean and we had a certain camaraderie. If being released from Merca had given me back my liberty, then being out at sea gave me my first opportunity to actually savour life again. The salt spray in my nostrils, the pitch and roll of the boat, the excitement and anticipation of hauling the catch on board, even the glare of the sun on the water all served to stir my island blood, and to round off an exhilarating day I then walked back to camp with a dozen fresh fish to be grilled over an open fire outside the hut that evening. What those fish were I have no idea, but the only thing stopping that meal being a gourmet perfection was the absence of a portion of chips.

It was clear that because we were not in uniform we were very much second-class citizens in Mombasa, so it was a relief when, after five long weeks, we finally received instructions to board a troopship heading home. The *Nea Hellas* was heading for Glasgow via Port Elizabeth, Cape Town and Gibraltar, stopping off in each port for a couple of days and letting us stretch our legs and look around a little. My favourite was Cape Town, as we managed to get to the top of Table Mountain and the locals were very sympathetic to our situation, standing us a beer or two and free cigarettes. I even got to meet a real celebrity while I was there, a great Dane the sailors called Nuisance who had been adopted by the navy and who was sent out to round up stragglers from the local bars. He was a huge dog who I first saw in Simonstown, where he was supposed to be living, though he also turned up in Cape Town, and I was told that we had something in common because he was an AB as well.

By the time we sailed from Cape Town I was starting to regain some of my strength. The troopship was only half-full for the final leg back to Britain, which made the passage feel almost like a holiday cruise until we were integrated into another convoy once we had made the open Atlantic. The realities of war were coming to the fore once again now we were nearing home, the U-Boat war was in full swing and it was with some relief that we finally stepped onto the quay at Glasgow docks in April, 1941.

It was hard to believe that it was only seven months since we had lost our ship, as it felt like enough had happened to fill seven years. Of course some of the boys we had shared our captivity with would never be coming home, and of the fove of us standing on the dockside Gibby was still wracked by back pain, though nothing was going to stop him heading for home. We couldn't afford to tarry long in Glasgow in any case, as we had very little money; I had scraped together five pounds sterling and had my travel voucher, so we headed straight off to the railway station and on to Aberdeen. The Granite City was freezing cold and wet, accentuating the cold greyness of the place and providing a strong contrast to the tropical climes we had recently left. The cold bit through us, partly due to lack of acclimatisation and partly due to being still very much underweight, but we boarded the *St. Clair*, bound for home, with broad smiles on our faces.

That evening I sat in the lounge as the ship ploughed her way north, sitting by myself, enjoying a beer and reflecting on recent events, when I suddenly began to shake, a shuddering tremor starting with my hands and running through my entire body, my teeth chattering uncontrollably. I have no idea whether this was a reaction to the change in weather or a psychological event linked to the fears and privations of the past few months. Certainly I wasn't dressed for a cold climate, the only clothes I now owned being the white cotton shirt, grey flannel trousers and checked sports jacket I had been given in Mombasa to replace the Italian army uniform which had not been deemed suitable for sightseeing in a British colony. I became very self-aware and more than a little embarrassed at this involuntary fit of shivering whilst in a public place, but I didn't think I would make it to my cabin without causing more of a spectacle, so I simply looked at the floor and hoped these deep, raking spasms would pass of their own accord. As I sat there gazing unhappily at my shoes I felt something being wrapped around my shoulders, and looked up to find my cousin Bob Mathieson's wife, Kathleen, putting her coat on my shaking frame. They had been sitting in another part of the bar and had been intending to come and speak, but had then noticed how I was shivering and my obvious discomfort, so Kathleen simply came over and performed her act of kindness without making any kind of fuss. Bob was also on his way home to Unst from his base in Malta where he was an officer in the RAF, so he had had plenty of stress of his own in recent months and recognised what he thought was a psychological reaction on my part. For five minutes I sat and shook, then waited a further ten for all trace of the tremors to subside until I felt strong and confident enough to stand up. I thanked Bob and Kathleen for sitting with me, thanked her for the use of her coat and after promising to meet up the next week took my leave and retired to my cabin. Once there I was overcome with utter exhaustion, closed my eyes and slept solidly until morning, not even noticing my cabin-mate returning during the night.

The next morning I exchanged the *St. Clair* for the old *Earl of Zetland* and thus made my way slowly north up the coast of Shetland until we finally docked at Baltasound in Unst at five o'clock in the afternoon. After managing to get a lift over Setter's Hill my first sight of home was an unforgettable experience, walking over the crest of the Buddabrake road and seeing the smoke from the chimney rising up towards a darkening sky

Recuperating back home following liberation and repatriation, 1941.

and smelling the unmistakable aroma of burning peat before the silhouette of the house itself came into view. Warmth, family and home were now no longer a distant wish but an immediate promise, just yards away and not over a distant horizon. As I entered through the kitchen door I was engulfed in a tide of elation and relief and felt my legs beginning to give way until Mother virtually carried me to a chair by the warm stove. Pleased as they were to see me they gave me the impression, as I mentioned before, that they had been confident I would return safely, but all I could do at the time was count my blessings at finally being able to relax in my own home with my own kith and kin around me. The evening passed in somewhat of a blur, but one piece of information that did filter through to my dazed brain was the news that we had recently totally routed the Italian army in north-east Africa who had made discretion the better part of valour and surrendered. I learned after the war that my treatment as a POW could have been far worse had I been captured in certain other parts of the world, but the news meant I went to bed with an even bigger grin on my face, wondering if Captain Bracco would be getting such a good night's sleep tonight.

I slept deeply and woke the next morning feeling stronger and fitter already, and Mother welcomed me downstairs with a hearty Shetland breakfast. As soon as I had finished I put on my boots and coat, collected the dogs from the barn and made my way down to the beach. The fresh smell of early spring was in the air, the crisp breeze blowing up the cliff carrying a tang of salt and seaweed, and the air was full of the cries of the nesting kittiwakes once again. I leaped from the bottom of the path to the loose stones at the head of the beach, feeling them rolling under my boots until I reached the soft, familiar give of the sand. The dogs ran on ahead as I became a boy once again, all the cares and worries dropping off me and being carried away on the tide as I resumed the pastime of an earlier life. The authorities had granted us one month's paid leave when we returned home, and I spent every day of it either beachcombing or fishing for trout, admittedly not being much help around the croft, although I don't think anybody was too concerned about that.

After a good four weeks of rest, fresh air and home cooking I felt strong enough to go back to work. A number of military buildings were under construction by the War Department at that time on Saxavord, the hill overlooking Burrafirth and the site of what would be Britain's most northerly early-warning radar system for many years to come, the weather domes later becoming an iconic image of Shetland's strategic importance in the "Cold War" with the Soviet bloc. I was given some labouring work which kept me occupied for the next six weeks, but as my strength returned so did my desire to resume my travels and get myself involved more directly with the war effort. The news had been good on my initial return, with the surrender of the Italians in Ethiopia, but since then there had been a succession of negative reports from various theatres of war around the world. First Yugoslavia and then Greece had fallen to the Germans; Rommel was leading his Afrika Corps to Egypt and as I was packing my bag to leave for Lerwick I heard the shocking news that Hitler's much-vaunted battleship, the *Bismarck*, had destroyed the pride of the Royal Navy, the *Hood*. This last item of news held the most pertinence for me, as it seemed that our merchant fleet would now be at the mercy of this sea-going monster as well as its U-boat cohorts, a situation that I heard might soon lead to Britain being starved out of the war. With the work on Saxavord nearing completion I had been asked if I could help out on the construction of a number of oil tanks being built in Lerwick, and I was happy to oblige. I was to lodge with a cousin in St. Sunniva Street and as I arrived at their house on a pleasant spring evening at the end of May the news was just coming over on the wireless that the Royal Navy had caught up with the *Bismarck* after all and sent her to the bottom. This was cause for celebration, so the night was passed in two or three of the Shetland capital's drinking establishments. I was not feeling so elated in the morning, however, as I started my new job a little worse for wear.

The work was mundane but probably what I needed at this time, helping me recuperate further and allowing me to spend weekends home with my family. I started off as a labourer but when, after a few months, the site cook left and there were no other volunteers, I donned my chef's hat. I felt I did reasonably well with my culinary efforts, though I'm not sure all my diners agreed. There were approximately forty men to feed and my duties included breakfast, lunch, evening meal and a licensed bar. The food was basic, mostly stews and soups, made from whatever ingredients were available at the time. It was edible most of the time, except for one occasion when one of the workers, encouraged by a group of local girls working at the nearby fish factory, laced the soup with epsom salts. The results were spectacular, with the entire workforce, including me, firstly making a dash for the two toilets available and then disappearing off in every direction seeking whatever other facilities may be available to a desperate man, including knocking on local residents' doors.

It took until the following evening for me to get over the worst effects of the salts, my constitution still being weaker than normal. This being the case, I thought that I might have a walk to the pub and try a pint. On the way I bumped into Edie, an Unst girl whom I had not seen since school, so greeted her warmly and gave her a kiss on the lips.

"You shouldn't have done that, Tom!" she said, drawing back.

"Why not – you're not going to get pregnant just from a kiss, are you?"

"No, but you're probably going to get measles if you haven't had it already!"

I hadn't noticed the spots that were starting to develop on her face and she told me that she had been diagnosed that afternoon and was heading home when she met me. My luck held true, and within a couple of days I was covered in spots and confined to my bed. And, of course, it was while I was laid up and feeling dreadful that I received notification to attend my medical prior to recruitment for the armed forces. The last thing I wanted was to be thought of as a draft dodger, so I dragged myself to the building being used for the medical assessments, still covered in angry, red spots. The medical centre was basically a stone-built hall with ill-fitting windows through which the wind howled incessantly. I took my place in the queue and removed all my clothing, being aware of those next to me in the line keeping what they hoped was a healthy distance once they had noticed the blotchy rash all over my body. The queue shuffled along slowly, and it was well over an hour later, by which time I felt fit to faint, when it was finally my turn to be examined. The doctor eyed me quizzically.

"What's all this, then?"

"Measles, sir," I replied, "I've had it about a week."

"You're an idiot, man! You should have stayed in your bed at least another week. Well, as you're here I suppose I'd better have a look at you."

Despite my illness and what the doctor thought of my mental capacity I passed the medical and was passed on to the recruiting officers. I had thought long and hard about what branch of the armed services I would like to serve in, so I made my way straight to the desk which handled applications for air-sea search and rescue. Working on the flying boats, searching for downed airmen or the survivors of ships which had been sunk really appealed to me, but to my disappointment there was a long waiting-list which was now closed for the foreseeable future. A sergeant from the tank corps approached me and told me they weren't getting many volunteers from Shetland; this didn't overly surprise me, as Shetlanders prefer to be on the ocean looking at a wide horizon than being locked like a sardine in a tin-box with a letter-box view of the world at best. I politely declined this invitation and made my way to the navy desk. The only vacancy at this time with any hope of receiving a call-up in the near future was aboard the minesweepers. The recruiting officer told me that this was a highly dangerous line of work to be in, but at least, I told myself, it's at sea, and I could see the tank corps sergeant still keeping an eye on me, so I signed up. I asked the officer if I should give up my current employment immediately and would I get a chance to spend a week or two at home before I commenced training?

To my surprise he said "Just keep on working as you are. It would surprise me if you heard anything at all in the next few months. We'll get hold of you when you're needed."

I left the recruiting office and stepped into the bright, afternoon sunlight with a sense of disappointment. I had vaguely thought that once I signed my name on the dotted line I would be whisked away with all speed to become a vital cog in a ruthlessly efficient war-machine. In fact I went back the building site and recommenced my cooking duties, never to hear another word from the navy regarding my chosen career clearing the sea lanes of "Hitler's hedgehogs".

Once the oil-tanks were completed I was instructed to pack my bags and travel to Orkney to work on a new major construction project which came to be known as the Churchill Barriers. Since the start of the First World War the Royal Navy had been using the natural harbour at Scapa Flow as a convenient base for operations against a German fleet based in the Baltic. At the beginning of World War Two the original defences were reinstated, incorporating sunken block ships to close the straits between five islands on the eastern side of the harbour, reinforced by booms and anti-submarine nets. Unfortunately the inadequacy of these defences was illustrated within weeks of the commencement of hostilities, when on 14th October, 1939, U-boat U-47 under the command of Günter Prien managed to navigate past the blockships on a high tide at night and torpedo HMS *Royal Oak* at her moorings, killing 833 of her crew.

In the wake of this disaster Winston Churchill, who was then First Lord of the Admiralty, paid a visit to Scapa Flow and within a couple of weeks had ordered the construction of four permanent barriers to close the passages and link together the five islands from Mainland in the north to South Ronaldsay in the south.

The work had been underway for nearly two years by the time I arrived to lend a hand, and the workforce was nearly 1,000 men. By the end of the year this number would double as Italian POW's arrived from the North African campaign and were set to work in a place very different from both their homeland and the arena they had been fighting in. Overhead cableways had to be constructed across the stretches of water concerned, from which wire cages were dropped containing broken rock from local quarries. These had to be guided into the water fairly accurately, as they then had a drop of sixty feet through a strong current before they came to rest on the bottom. Once these were down they were covered in concrete blocks, weighing up to ten tons, which were required to withstand the ferocity of the sea as well as the U-boat threat. These blocks were constructed locally, ferried in by lorry and off-loaded near the work-sites. We would then load them by crane onto our own trucks when they were required before being loaded onto barges which would hopefully deposit them at their intended position. The work was quite monotonous and repetitive, though there were often comic moments of light relief which usually centred on my efforts to get the Italian workers who were already there to understand what they were supposed to be doing. They were willing workers who mostly seemed pleased to be anywhere away from the front line, and I didn't hold the circumstances of my former incarceration against them. They lived mainly in camps on Burray and Lamb Holm which they made as comfortable as possible, even constructing their own chapel, while most of the British workers, including myself, stayed in and around the capital, Kirkwall. The people of Orkney were a friendly lot both to us and the POW's, but after three months of hard labour on the barriers I was getting restless to get back to sea, so decided to pursue any opportunities that might come my way in that direction.

On a particularly hot day in mid-August I was working on one of the barges dropping off the blocks when I noticed a tug steaming into the bay and tying up alongside a pier only a couple of hundred yards away. Once we had dropped the last block the barge headed back to shore, and as it was now lunchtime I decided to pay the tugboat skipper a visit and see if he had any vacancies. This was the *Gatville*, a French boat that had crossed the channel in 1940 when the invading Germans had completed their invasion of France, and had been put back to work by the British. By a stroke of luck they were short of a fireman, and once he had heard what experience I had at sea the skipper offered me the job there and then.

"Don't worry about not having done the job before," he said, "we'll teach you all you need to know – you'll soon pick it up!"

I didn't need telling twice, and hurried off to tell the foreman that I would be leaving on the next tide. He wasn't exactly thrilled at the news, but very fairly agreed to make up my cards and within an hour had paid me all that I was still owed. It was a wonderful feeling to be getting back to sea again even if I wouldn't be undertaking any long-distance journeys on this particular vessel, but there were still plenty of dangers lurking for any ship in the waters around the British Isles at that time. The U-boat threat was ever-present, mines were laid in the approaches to all the main ports and German aircraft still roved the skies looking for easy targets. Things were still going very much in Germany and her ally Japan's favour at this point in the war, with the German army advancing on the eastern front in Russia, Rommel rampaging around the desert in North Africa and the Japanese capturing numerous island-groups in the Pacific. In contrast, when I stepped aboard my new place of work, the skipper told me of a rumour that an invasion force of ours had already landed in France and we may be heading urgently to the south coast, although it later transpired that this was the ill-fated Dieppe raid which lasted less than a day and ended in disaster, with more than a thousand of the six thousand force being killed.

I picked up the role of fireman in very short time, most of the job being known to me already, although I found raking the fires out an extremely arduous task to begin with. Once I became physically accustomed to the work it was just a case of putting up with the heat and noise when working in the bowels of the ship.

After completing our tasks in Orkney we made our way back to the Scottish mainland and from there down the east coast to Hull, where we were due a refit. We were six weeks ashore in Hull, generally relaxing and enjoying the late summer weather, with just the odd German bomber making nuisance raids to remind us that there was still a war on. After this we continued south, eventually making our base at Southsea on the Hampshire coast. Most of our work now centred on the south of England, towing barges between London and the coastal ports surrounding Southampton and Portsmouth. I took up residence in digs in Southsea and worked solidly through to August, 1943, when the *Gatville* had another partial refit and I took the chance to take some leave and visit home for the first time in a year. My brother Johnnie was home as well, so we made the most of our time together, spending most of it fishing. One day we out at the mouth of Burrafirth, dropping lines in the lee of the cliffs of Saxavord, when I heard a commotion in the water and saw large air bubbles rising from the depths about a hundred yards off the port bow. I called out to Johnny and as he turned to look a long, dark shape emerged from the waves and sat bobbing on the surface, causing us to quickly pull our lines in and look at each other anxiously.

"What the hell kind of a sub is that?"

Although it was obvious what manner of craft had appeared before us, it was far smaller than any submarine I had ever seen before, being approximately fifty feet long. To begin with there was no movement from within, so we started rowing towards it, hoping it wasn't an enemy craft. When we were within twenty feet a hatch opened in the slightly raised centre-section, and a smiling face topped by a naval cap popped up.

"Hello chaps, hope we didn't alarm you – how's the fishing?"

Our unexpected visitor was in fact a midget submarine carrying a crew of four, based somewhere on the west coast of Scotland. The skipper didn't give much away, although he did say that they would be making a trip over to Norway. I didn't know if they were on their way already or if they were training for the trip, but on being invited to come aboard and have a look round I politely declined. She didn't appear to sit on the water too comfortably, and I had a vision of pulling the thing over as I clambered aboard and sending it straight to the bottom. The officer was a very friendly man, and handed Johnny and myself a cigarette each, while he lit one for himself. Apparently it was off limits to smoke in the cramped confines of the submarine, so he made sure that there were frequent "rest-stops" where he could top-up his nicotine levels and even occasionally have a chat with the odd startled fisherman. I believe that this was one of the famous X craft, midget submarines built to attack the *Tirpitz* in her lair in Ka fjord in Norway, of whom a number were lost both in the attack and on the long journey there from Scotland, under tow by conventional submarines. Personally speaking I wouldn't have wanted to cross the Thames in one, never mind the North Sea, and I have often wondered if the crew of the one we had our encounter with survived the mission. We finished our cigarettes and reached over to shake hands with the skipper, wishing him good luck, seeing the sub disappearing into the depths once more as we pulled for home.

Two weeks later I was back on the *Gatville* once more, though still waiting to be called up for minesweeper service; the next nine months were spent pushing and pulling barges from place to place around the coast and were mostly uneventful, although no time spent at sea in wartime can be described as stress-free. The general mood in the country had changed by this time, and with our American allies we seemed to be pushing the Germans and Japanese back in every theatre of the war. Ever since we had arrived in Southsea in 1942 we had noticed a lot of activity in the surrounding area involving both troops and equipment, and this seemed to intensify from the beginning of 1944. The seafront at Southsea was a restricted zone, part of a coastal strip that later in 1944 ran from The Wash in Norfolk to Lands End in Cornwall and which was closed to all casual visitors. We were issued with special passes to let us continue operating in the area, and virtually all of our work was now for the military. Every time we landed now, whether it was Portsmouth, Southampton or any of the other south coast ports, we seemed to hear more and more American accents. We didn't mind this at all as it was good to know that they were on our side and they raised our spirits with their bullish outlook, outspoken with their confident predictions of victory, seemingly always eager to get to grips with the enemy. By late spring all movement in the region, whether at sea or on land, was severely restricted, and the locals we spoke to in the Southsea pub we frequented told us that Hampshire was now virtually one vast military camp.

It was obvious that something big was imminent and we knew that the only possible reason for this vast gathering of forces was the invasion of France. As May turned to June the tension at all points along the south coast became palpable, more and more ships were arriving, men and machinery were gathering and there was the feeling of an unstoppable momentum building. By now we were working flat-out, manoeuvring ships, barges, pontoons and anything else that floated into position for whatever the grand plan decreed, and were also spending more of our time as messengers for the gathering fleet, as radio communication was kept to a minimum.

Saturday, 3rd June and Sunday the 4th saw us shuttling between the ships that were sheltering in the lee of the Isle of Wight and out as far east as Selsey Bill, delivering "final orders" for their tasks and positions in the invasion fleet. Once this last job was completed we were to head back to Portsmouth, take in tow six ammunition barges and wait in readiness to resupply one of the warships. Obviously we were still not privy to any official information, but it was clear that the invasion was imminent and we expected to see the whole assorted flotilla head out on the morning of the 4th June. More ships were appearing all day from both east and west, but as the day wore on the steady flow of smaller vessels and landing craft into the ports increased and there appeared to be a real log-jam of ships outside the harbour stretching off to Bembridge on the east coast of the Isle of Wight. By evening it was evident that few boats were stirring from their moorings and those already at sea were doing little more than holding their stations, so by the time we bedded down at some time past midnight we were still speculating on when the operation would get under way. We had been asked to stay on board that night in anticipation of being required for urgent messaging duties in the early hours of the following morning, so the whole crew had grabbed a blanket each and curled up in whatever space we could find below decks when we moored up at Southsea. There was no sleeping outside as the weather had been getting worse all day; we couldn't see the smaller craft getting outside the harbour without foundering, so we guessed that it was now just a waiting game.

I must have immediately fallen into a deep slumber as the next thing I recall is the chief engineer shaking me awake at 3.30am on Monday morning. I took a quick look out on deck for some fresh air, clutching a mug of hot tea, but could see very little as it was still a long time before dawn and the sky was overcast. I then hurried back down to the engine room and helped the chief get the engines going before *Gatville* resumed her duties scuttling between the shore and the ships, delivering what must now be very last-minute orders. Even below decks I could sense that other engines were turning that morning and that the mighty fleet was now coming to life. The next chance I got to stretch my legs was at 8am, and now there really was a sight to see; we had sailed west along the Solent and were just now passing a mile or so off the Needles on the west extremity of the Isle of Wight, in the company of what looked like at least a thousand vessels. On the far horizon I saw warships of all sizes, battleships, cruisers, destroyers, frigates and minesweepers, both British and American, while closer to us sailed a variety of other craft, with troop transports and landing craft mingling with armed trawlers, and motor launches and tugboats like ourselves weaving amongst them. We appeared to be playing the part of escort to a line of large landing craft carrying tanks and other armoured vehicles, as I could see the turrets above the bulwarks, and every vessel was sailing south. The fleet was fragmenting as the faster ships drew ahead of the slower, and as the unwieldy-looking landing craft hit open water beyond the lee of the Isle of Wight they began to roll in a manner that looked uncomfortable in the extreme and made me hope that they were all good sailors aboard. Spitfires and other fighters flew overhead, keeping watch over all that was happening on the ocean, but I never caught sight of an enemy warplane that whole day.

As a fireman I was kept busy below deck for the majority of the day, only getting the odd rare glimpse of the outside world, so it was very difficult for me to keep track of where we travelled amongst the fleet and who we carried our messages to and from. By evening there was nothing for me to do below, so the chief told me that we were heading for home and to take a breather and get some fresh air. As I climbed the ladder to the deck the deep throbbing of heavy marine engines came through the clear night air, resonating down the hatch and through the superstructure. The sound was impressive, but the sight was just as awesome, as even more ships filled the sea, still steaming south to the Normandy coast of France, while we retraced our steps towards the mouth of the Solent.

As the light faded the fleet was no more than ghostly silhouettes drifting through the deepening darkness, not a light showing on any of them, though some bore down closely upon us before speeding past and leaving us watching their bright, phosphorescent wake. I would never have believed that so many ships could occupy the same stretch of ocean at night, with not a light to be seen or a klaxon to be heard, and all moving with a common purpose towards an unknown destiny. We were making our way back through what must be the mightiest fleet ever assembled, and we knew that by morning the landing on the enemy shore would be underway. By 12.30am on the morning of 6th June we were approaching our home pontoon and we could hear the drone of aircraft above the clouds heading out across the water, which I later learnt were the transport aircraft carrying parachutists and bombers towing gliders full of more airborne troops.

That morning we were woken at 5.30, and even before we got underway we could hear the percussion of heavy guns being fired from many miles distant and the drone of aircraft passing overhead. We were assigned to re-supply HMS *Erebus*, a monitor that had been built in the First World War for the very purpose of supporting land-based operations, having a shallow draft to allow her to operate close inshore. She had had a refit in 1939 and was now part of the Western Task Force, supporting the American landings on Utah beach and bombarding the German coastal batteries at Barfleur. She was capable of firing a 15-inch shell over twenty miles inland if required. She sailed back towards Portsmouth in the early evening of 7th June, having expended her entire arsenal in one day. There was no room for her to dock at the quayside so we were tasked to manoeuvre the six barges crammed full of high explosive ammunition through the busy harbour traffic and park them up alongside her. Her crew would then get to work in transferring the cargo on board the old warship, working quickly and expertly so that she could cast off the empty barges within a few hours and steam straight back out of the harbour. She would then race at top speed back to her appointed position and resume her bombardment of the German defenders. This routine continued for more than two months, the *Erebus* taking on six barges of ammo every two days as she pounded

Above: HMS Erebus ready to depart for Normany beachs. (Courtesy of Navyphotos)
Below: D-Day. (Courtesy of www.combinedops.com)

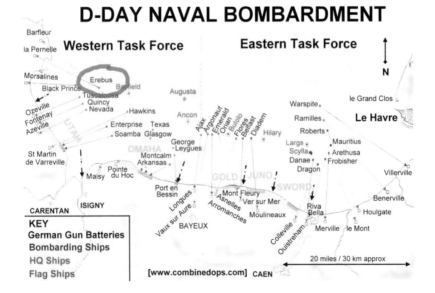

the French coast. In between re-supplying *Erebus* we would perform other minor duties in and around the harbour, including re-arming other, smaller, warships but always had to be ready for *Erebus* without a moment's delay. By August she was moving east along the coast and by 10th August was bombarding the German forces defending Le Havre. Here she was engaged in a duel with a battery of three 170mm K18 guns based at Clos des Ronces and sustained sufficient damage to have to return to the dockyard for repairs.

One evening in late June we tied up in Southsea after having re-supplied *Erebus* and seen her steam away once again. It had been a busy day for the *Gatville*, but now as I strolled back to my digs the sky was clear, there was a warm breeze blowing in off the sea and an air of tranquillity seemed to be descending with the fading of the day. My routine was to pop into the local pub, the Waverley Arms I seem to remember, for a pint on the way home, though if there was company this sometimes stretched to two or three. The landlady, Grace, had taken a liking to me and often gave me a drink "on the house", so I knew there was always a welcome waiting for me. The pub was on the seafront and had a splendid view out across the Solent to the Isle of Wight and beyond. Grace was behind the bar as usual as I entered, with the normal smattering of locals and dock workers spread around the saloon.

"Evening Jock, busy day?"

"Just the usual, Grace," I replied, always being careful not to mention anything specific about my duties when I was ashore, "pint of bitter please."

I tasted the frothy head of the ale with relish before working my way to the body of the pint, and stayed chatting with Grace at the bar. Half an hour passed, and as I finished the drink I decided to pop to the toilet before continuing my journey home. As I washed my hands I began to hear a low rumble coming from somewhere outside the pub; an engine noise, and growing louder, but not one that I could immediately identify. As I stood at the sink listening to the sinister droning the door of the gents suddenly slammed open and Grace burst in. Without any explanation or apology she grabbed my hand and dragged me towards the door.

"Quick Jock, come and see this!"

As we exited the pub we found the entire clientele gathered on the road outside, eyes all fixed on an object which was approaching fast from the sea and about two thousand feet up. It looked like a small aeroplane, but seemed to be flying in a somewhat different manner to any other plane I had ever seen, and sounded like nothing I had heard before. This, then, was the source of the undulating droning sound, though I had absolutely no idea what it was I was looking at.

"It's a 'Doodlebug'," said Grace, as if reading my thoughts.

"I've heard of them, but what is it exactly?"

"A flying bomb. I've been told that it's nothing to worry about as long as the engine doesn't stop, but if it does, throw yourself down flat on the ground. I think they're being aimed at London."

It only took a few seconds for the aircraft to reach us, and we had a grandstand view as it passed overhead. I could see that there was no cockpit for a pilot, and no propellers. As it crossed the coast and headed further inland there was a glow in the gathering murk from its exhaust which suggested that it travelled by some kind of rocket power – none of us there had heard of the jet engine at that time. As we filtered back into the pub there was much speculation about what effect this new phenomenon would have on the course of the war. It was, of course, the V1, the first of Hitler's promised "super-weapons", and it certainly lived up to the other of its nicknames, the "buzz-bomb". It sounded like a giant, angry wasp as it approached, and the low, pulsing sound travelled for miles. It made the hair stand up on the back of your neck when you heard it, so I could only imagine the effect it would have if you heard the noise cut out and could only wait helplessly for it to fall to earth and detonate. I didn't realise at the time but I would later experience a very similar feeling when I was stationed in London.

The other immediate topic of conversation among the regulars was how Grace had rushed straight into the gents and reappeared dragging me behind her, causing some ribald comments and a few raised eyebrows in jest; I pretended to have been shocked at the time as well and the landlady of the pub turned a decent shade of scarlet before she saw the funny side and had a laugh about it herself.

BORN A BEACHCOMBER

Chapter Eight

By September 1944 our workload had returned to normal and as I was due some leave I decided to take the road north once again to visit home. My brother Johnny was working on a block ship in Leith at that time and living with our cousin Bella once more, so I thought I would stop off with them for a day or two to break my journey. A block ship was to be sailed out to the entrance of the docks and sunk there to prevent the enemy gaining access to the harbour in an emergency such as imminent invasion. As the British and American forces were by now getting close to the borders of Germany itself I thought it very unlikely that our enemies would be able to mount an invasion of Edinburgh, but Johnny was enjoying living in Leith for the time being and he had a good knowledge of everything happening in the dock area. As we sat in the pub that evening he mentioned that a War Department boat was in the docks and he believed they were looking for crew, though he had no idea where they were bound or what the nature of their work was. I mulled the idea over that night, and by morning had decided to try my luck with the mysterious War Department vessel. I was keen to get back to a deck job and out of the boiler room and wanted to get more involved in the war effort again, as the south coast was a lot quieter now that the initial invasion was over. It seemed like everything was happening just out of sight over the horizon and this might even get me over to France.

Next morning I walked down to the docks and explained my intentions to the dock master at the gates who then issued me with a pass. Although my acquaintance with the vessel was destined to be short-lived and I cannot recall her name, the skipper saw me straight away and after I had given him details of my work experience he offered me the one remaining deck-hand's job. This was too good an offer to turn down so I accepted there and then, which was a good job as they were sailing the following day, though it meant that I would have to forego my two weeks leave. The boat was not large, no more than six hundred tons, but it could have been the *Ark Royal* by the size of the smile on my face as I bounded back down the gangplank to head off and collect my belongings from Bella's. I shook hands with Johnny and my cousins once more, wrote a quick note to my family in Unst apologising for not arriving home as promised and just about ran all the way back to the boat.

We made ready for sailing that night and left on the morning tide, bound for London. The sun was shining and the breeze was fresh in my face, no more fires to tend and the promise of the unknown beckoning. Life was all about new challenges and new experiences, but unfortunately the one I was about to have was not the experience I had had in mind. After two days sailing I began to feel unwell, which at first I put down to a stomach bug, but which saw me go rapidly downhill to a point where I was unable to stand and had to be confined to my bunk. The medical officer and the skipper were concerned about me and told me that I would have to be hospitalised when we reached London. As luck would have it there was thick fog across the Thames estuary when we arrived at Southend, so there was nothing for it but to tie up and wait, which we did for three days, with me all the while laid in my bunk feeling alternately feverishly hot or freezing cold and little better than death warmed up.

At last the fog lifted and we were able to continue up the Thames until we eventually reached our destination, Woolwich in south-east London. At the pier an ambulance was waiting to transport me to the Dreadnought Seamen's Hospital in Greenwich where I was put into an isolation room until they had discovered the cause of my ill-health. The diagnosis turned out to be yellow jaundice which I had thought was a tropical disease, but the doctor told me I had an infection in my liver which may have been caused by something as simple as a bad pint of beer. The treatment would be lengthy, possibly six weeks, and I would need to stay in hospital for the duration followed by a similar period of convalescence. My first thought was that I would lose my new, highly-prized job, but there was obviously nothing for it but to follow doctor's orders, and in any case I was in no fit state to argue. The first two weeks in hospital passed in a fevered blur, but by the third week I was able to take note of my surroundings as my condition gradually improved. I had been left in my isolation ward all this time, which was situated on the top floor of the hospital and gave a good view down towards the river and docklands. The hospital itself was an old, austere building which had changed its function from looking after Royal Navy personnel to merchant seamen in the late nineteenth century.

Prior to this merchant sailors in need of hospital treatment had been catered for in three hospital ships moored in the river off Greenwich, and the hospital took its name from the last of them, the *Dreadnought*. It had suffered bomb damage during the air-raids of the early 1940s though it was the attacks of the present that concerned me. The population of London was well-used to the blackout by now and observed it fastidiously, but the night would still be illuminated with sudden flashes of light that illustrated the fact that the Nazis still had the city in their sights

The jaundice was very debilitating and would leave me feeling exhausted for hours at a time, during which I could do nothing but sleep. My normal sleep pattern was totally disrupted, and as a consequence I would usually find myself sleeping through the day and staying awake for at least part of the night. It was on those nights that I would sit up by the window, listening for the pulsating, now unmistakable throbbing of the doodlebug motor and watching for the glare as the high explosive detonations lit up the city north and south of the river. The noise of detonation would always follow slightly after the explosive flash, and would mingle with the booming of the big guns situated in the parks and open heath nearby. Smoke would drift across the leaden grey rooftops and the burning fires would be curiously magnified through the haze, giving the impression of far greater devastation than was actually taking place, though the reality was bad enough. Once, when everything appeared quiet in the early hours of the morning, I saw a sheet of flame suddenly race into the sky, followed by a terrific crack of thunder as a house took a direct hit a couple of streets away and disintegrated. I later learned that this was the V2, the world's first ballistic missile, developed by Germany as one of Hitler's wonder weapons which he believed would strike terror into the allied nations and turn the tide the war in his favour. Unlike the doodlebug the V2 came silently, falling from fifty miles up at a speed faster than sound to deliver a warhead packed with explosive, but rather than terrify and cow the population it became another example of Hitler's miscalculations about the spirit of the British people, with none of the mass hysteria hoped for by the Germans, though nearly three thousand were killed in the few months that it was targeted on England.

Those weeks spent watching the tortures that London suffered gave me a profound respect for the city-folk who bore the brunt of the onslaught on the home islands but never once seemed to contemplate capitulation. Being at sea in a merchant ship during World War Two meant waiting for an unseen death to strike at any moment, with very little to fight back with. The same could be said of the civilian population of the capital. Londoners had no safe port at the end of a voyage but would have to live under constant threat until the war was virtually over. After six weeks the doctors decided that I was strong enough to leave the hospital, so I was packed off to a convalescent home near Woking in Surrey. The fresh air and the delightful gardens of the home were a total contrast to the dark, Victorian surroundings of the hospital in Greenwich and both physically and spiritually I improved in leaps and bounds. A further six weeks saw me pronounced cured and fit enough to go back to work, so after a phone call from the War Office to confirm that I was still gainfully employed I packed my bag once more and headed back to London.

The ship I had joined at Leith had taken on another deck-hand at Woolwich and left on its next mission. I had been worried that the War Office would forget about me, but there was a position for me on a yacht called the *Shangri-La* based at Westminster Pier. When I arrived at the pier I found waiting for me one of the most beautiful boats I had ever seen; over sixty feet from prow to stern, a sloop made of shining teak and brilliantly polished brass fittings. She had been a millionaire's plaything before the war and been sequestered by the War Department at the time of the Dunkirk evacuation, though I never found out if she had actually sailed to France at that time or not. The crew were all about my age and friendly with it, comprising the skipper Charlie Hornby, the engineer Len Simpson and Ronny Cox, my fellow deck-hand. I was issued with a smart naval uniform and informed that the *Shangri-La* was being used to ferry top military personnel, both navy and army, between central London and other bases down-river and along the south coast. When we were not employed on these duties she was used as a convalescent activity for wounded servicemen, and it was these trips that I enjoyed the most, when they would spend two or three nights aboard and we would take them down-river to Sheerness or up-river as far as Wargrave. Most of them – and us – had never experienced this kind of luxury before, the cabins done out like staterooms, with sumptuous fitted carpets underfoot, sprung mattresses on the beds and elaborate gold fittings everywhere, and we made sure they felt like royalty when they were on board.

The war was progressing very much in our favour now and it was clear that the Axis powers would not be able to sustain their war efforts and delay victory for the Allies for very much longer. I was happy with the work I was doing, although I frustrated at having so little direct involvement in the war effort and it was obvious that my call-up to minesweeper duty would not be happening before the end of the conflict. By April 1945 Londoners were at last able to sleep peacefully in their beds without the fear of death falling from the skies, as the advancing British and American armies over-ran the airfields and launch sites that put the south of England within reach of the Nazi bombers and 'V' weapons. If the western forces were advancing rapidly then the Russian armies seemed to be positively racing into the Third Reich from the east, knocking at the very door of the German capital itself. At the beginning of May there was a sudden and surreal announcement that Hitler was dead, quickly followed by news of the fall of Berlin, and finally on 8th May came the news that we had all been waiting for but hardly dared believe: Germany had surrendered. We happened to be tied up at Westminster as the news came through, and as we weren't due to take any passengers on board for the next few days Charlie, the skipper told us: "Bugger off and enjoy yourselves!"

We made the yacht fast, battened down the hatches and scrambled up the ladder to the pier, joining the thronging crowds who were making their way along Whitehall. It was a frenzy of smiling, cheering, faces, the elation tempered with relief that it was over at last; and the thought that we were the lucky ones who were still alive and that we had defeated a deadly enemy. I was in the right place at just the right time to see Winston Churchill, the great man himself, appear on a balcony above our heads and speak to the crowd, but I don't recall a word he said, probably due to my own euphoria and the great cheer that went up as soon as he was seen. After he had spoken I was then swept along with the crowd, like a great ocean current, pouring out into Trafalgar Square and veering left, flowing through Admiralty Arch and not stopping until I found myself washed up in front of Buckingham Palace itself. We cheered, and carried on cheering until the French doors to the balcony were flung open and the King and Queen appeared, along with Winston once again, though how he had negotiated the crowds and managed to get here before us I had no idea. It seemed the entire population of London was squeezed into the area in front of the palace, and as the royal family appeared in front of us I believe that every hat in London was thrown into the air. The pent-up outpourings of a nation burst forth that day, and I don't believe that Britain has seen such heart-felt celebrations either before or since. I spent the rest of that wonderful day simply going with the flow of the crowd, being invited to share a family's sandwiches in St. James' Park, having a bottle of stout thrust into my hand in Leicester Square, until I returned to the yacht at about six o'clock that evening. I was pretty much exhausted by then, but no sooner had I set foot on the deck than Len and Ronny appeared, freshly shaved and hair slicked down.

"Come on, Tom, they're having a dance outside the pub across the river. I don't think they've got any music yet, so why don't you bring your gramophone, just in case?"

There was a pub at the far end of Westminster Bridge; I forget the name now, but we used it as our local when we were moored at the pier. The party was being organised on a bomb site next door, so I grabbed my little wind-up gramophone and a few records and made my way over. It had only cost me a shilling second-hand but it turned out to be a good investment, as others brought more records from their houses nearby and it ended up playing for the rest of the night. I probably danced with a hundred girls that night and certainly drank my share, until eventually I felt that I'd had enough and wandered off in the direction of the bridge. As I reached it I noticed a lone figure standing in the middle, staring off into the distance down-river. It was a London bobby, still on duty and unable to join in the wild celebrations, so, on the spur of the moment, I went back to the pub and bought a dram of whisky, taking it out to the guardian on the bridge.

"Here you go pal, have one on me."

"Sorry, son" he replied, "I never touch a drop when I'm on duty. I'm happy enough, anyway, but thanks for the thought."

So I had one final drink on the day that we won a war, standing on a bridge in the heart of the nation's capital with the river flowing darkly beneath. I never saw my gramophone again, but it had served its purpose that night, and I had the consolation the next morning of waking up to a continent at peace.

Our pleasant existence on the *Shangri-La* carried on after the end of the war much the same as before, until one day late in the autumn of 1945. We had been refuelling and re-supplying downriver at Woolwich and arrived back at Westminster pier in the early evening. Normally we cooked all our meals onboard, but as it was a nice, warm evening we decided to go ashore and find a restaurant for a change. We had changed into "civvies" and were just setting off along the pier when we heard the gurgling rush of water entering the boat from some point unseen, so we rushed back aboard, scrambled down below decks and quickly lifted the floorboards. Sure enough the dirty river water was creeping up in the bilges, so we cast off the moorings, started the motor and I took the wheel to head her off across to the far side of the river. Just below Westminster Bridge and above County Buildings there was an area of flat mud where I thought I could beach her, and as the tide was in I managed to drive her right up to the high water mark just as the engine compartment flooded and the motor cut out. The boat settled down on an even keel on the mud flat. We made her fast ashore, put an anchor light up on the mast and made our way back over the bridge to Westminster pier. The harbour master and a salvage crew arrived the next morning at low water to inspect the damage, which unfortunately was extensive, the entire hull below the water-line being riddled with rot. It was decided that she was not repairable, and the last we saw of our Shangri-La was the sad sight of her heading down-river in a driftwood barge to be broken up.

A week after the demise of the *Shangri-La* we were despatched to Dover to pick up her replacement. This was the motor-launch *Barham*, which had a fibreglass hull and a powerful engine capable of pushing her to twenty-five knots and more. The *Shangri-La* had been a wonderful boat to sail in but the *Barham* was altogether more practical and efficient. We were able to carry our wounded forces personnel to a far greater variety of places and in far less time, which meant we virtually doubled our work capability. Westminster pier was no longer suitable as a mooring site for the new boat, so we now mainly tied up at Cadogan pier in Chelsea, an affluent, residential area of central London. Life carried on as normal until the springtime of 1946, when we were ordered down-river to Woolwich reach for two weeks of training, mooring up each night at the Woolwich harbour service pier. One evening Charlie, Ronnie and I decided to go out for a spot of fresh air and a meal, and ended up in a local restaurant in Woolwich on the south side of the Thames. I was halfway through my meal when two very smartly dressed girls came in and sat at a table near the doorway. One of them caught my eye immediately, very slim with long, auburn hair, sitting chatting intently with her friend and taking no notice of anyone else in the restaurant. I knew immediately that if I didn't summon up the nerve to at least talk to her I would regret it later, so I got up and approached the girls table in as nonchalant a manner as I could manage.

"Good evening ladies, can I buy you something to eat?"

They looked at each other and I thought they were about to laugh out-loud, but they managed to contain their mirth and the auburn-haired one replied politely, "No thanks, we ate earlier."

Things weren't looking promising, but I wasn't going to be put off that easily.

"A cup of tea, then?"

She looked up and probably felt a bit sorry for me, as her gaze softened and she said "OK then. One cup of tea won't hurt."

I didn't need another invitation, so at this I pulled a chair up to their table and my two pals came over and joined us as well. The girls were called Hilda and Doreen, both local London girls, who were good-humoured enough to put up with the three of us for an hour or so, before they said they had to go. Once again I decided to chance my arm, and asked Hilda if she would let me walk her home.

"Alright Tom," she replied, "but you may regret it, because it's quite a way and it's all uphill."

Hilda lived in Mayhill Road in Charlton – a good thirty minute walk from the restaurant in Woolwich – with her parents and three brothers. She had stayed in London throughout the war, working in Johnson and Phillips, a local cable manufacturing factory whose products were vital to the war effort, particularly to Britain's aircraft industry. The river and the docks were not far away, and the area was bombed intensely throughout the war, so Hilda spent most nights sleeping in the Anderson shelter at the bottom of the garden. I was shocked when we arrived at Hilda's road,

Johnson and Phillips Ltd., electrical cabling factory, Charlton, SE London, early 1941 (at the height of the Blitz), Hilda fourth from left.

because only the two ends were still standing, with the middle of the road just a jumble of rubble.

"Most of that was a single landmine that came down one night," she explained. "We were lying in the shelter when all hell broke loose, and we were sure that our own house must have gone.

"We didn't leave the shelter until dawn, when we found our house intact with a few others at the bottom of the road, and a dozen or so at the top, but a lot of our neighbours were killed or injured."

Another time a bomb had fallen in the road outside her house, and the back of her piano bore the scars made by hundreds of glass fragments as the windows were blown in. Fortunately no-one had been in the front sitting room at the time. Nothing would make the Harris family pack up and leave, though, and I was amazed then, as already mentioned, at the resilience of the London folk who toughed it out during the Blitz. Hilda did her bit working at the factory, even though she had trained as a pianist and her father had encouraged her to become a music teacher. Her brothers were all serving in the armed forces; the eldest, Cyril, had been a professional soldier at the outbreak of war, serving in the Kings Royal Rifles, which had been their father's regiment in the First World War. He was a regimental boxing champion, had escaped from a German POW camp and served in the Eighth Army under Montgomery in North Africa. He was a proper action-man, but unfortunately by the time I met him he was suffering from a brain tumour as a result of a direct hit on his tank during the North African campaign, and would only survive for one more year. Stan had spent the war with the RAF in East Africa, based in Mombasa in Kenya, while Reg had joined the Royal Berkshire Regiment, initially stationed in India. He had been part of the force that had met the Japanese army thrust at the borders of India, halted their advance after savage fighting and eventually pursued them across and out of Burma, being one of the first to march into Rangoon. Reg fought alongside the Gurkhas in Burma, and gained a profound respect for their fighting prowess. By the time he was de-mobbed he was a hard-bitten veteran of jungle warfare, used to fighting with both the rifle and the Gurkha Kukri and had been promoted to Colour Sergeant, yet he was still only twenty-two years old. By 1946 he had joined the War Office as a civil servant and had been sent to Germany to help in the post-war reconstruction of that country, while Stan had found employment as an accountant with a city wine merchant.

Though we came from very different worlds I decided that I had met the girl for me, and so started a courtship that lasted only three months,

Hilda, aged 21, 1940.

Thomas and Hilda on their wedding day, Greenwich, 1946.
Below with Barham *crew members. From left: Ronny Cox,*
Thomas, Hilda, Charlie Hornby, Len Simpson

and a marriage that has lasted sixty-seven years and counting. Though the distance between us was not that great in terms of miles, Hilda lived in a part of London that was not easily accessible from the centre of town where I was staying at Cadogan pier. I would catch a train and two or three buses to reach her house of an evening, but would invariably find that I had missed the last connection by the time I had dropped her off and was ready to head back to the boat. This meant I would have to walk back, which I would do several times a week, leaving Charlton at midnight and arriving in Chelsea at dawn. Though I was young and fit in those days I realised that this was not the ideal scenario, so after three months I gained the blessing of her parents, asked her to marry me and much to my delight she accepted. We were married in the registrar's office in Woolwich on 27th July 1946, Hilda having her family and friends attending while my only guests were Charlie, Ronnie and Les from the *Barham*; my brothers Willie and Johnny had returned to work on the croft in Shetland after the war, and there was no money for any of the family to make the long journey south. My eldest brother Alex was a lighthouse keeper based on the Scottish mainland at that time, but his period of leave didn't coincide with the planned date of the wedding, so I just had to get on with it without any support from home.

Not long after Hilda and I had started our married life together the War Office decided that the *Barham*'s current duties were no longer called for, so the crew was disbanded and split up between other vessels. Ronnie and I found ourselves transferred to a boat towing targets for army gunnery practice, stationed on the south coast at Dover. If we thought the *Barham* was fast after the *Shangri-La*, then the new boat the *Bethune* was another step up, her three powerful engines capable of pushing her to over forty-five knots. We spent the first week getting used to the handling of the new boat and the sheer exhilaration of its turn of speed, practicing with the target being pulled behind, letting it out to four hundred yards in good visibility and six hundred in misty or cloudy conditions. The new crew gelled well together, and after a week it was decided that we were well drilled enough to allow live ammunition to be fired in our direction. Up to that point I had no idea what we would be letting ourselves in for and no idea how accurate the shooting was likely to be. In fact the marksmanship of the soldiers was normally remarkably good; the aim for the gunners was to fire close by the target as it sped up and down in front of them, but sometimes they'd get bored with this and try to score a few direct hits. We kept hammers, nails and spare planking on board to deal with minor repairs, but a good direct hit would blow the target out of the water and leave us collecting scraps of driftwood to take back as evidence of their accuracy.

On one particular day there was driving rain and a howling gale that was reducing visibility considerately, so we streamed the target out to maximum distance and waited for the army officer on board to give them the order to fire. As soon as he did so we heard the whoosh of shells coming in our direction, followed by two large plumes of water as the detonations straddled our craft, probably no more than twenty feet off either side. They were obviously mistaking us for the target in the choppy swell and we all knew by now that the first two shots were normally range-finders. As the boat began weaving and the crew were keeping as low as possible, flinching with the thought of what was coming next, the officer desperately tried to make contact with the on-shore radio operator. Luckily he managed to cancel the next salvo, and the airwaves were blue for the next ten minutes as our officer conveyed his thoughts as to the competency of the gun crew. He ordered us to wind in the target and head for shore, as he was keen to follow up on his wireless broadside with another one face to face with his men. We were just happy to still be floating in one piece on the sea rather than blown into matchwood and just as happy not to be part of the company of gunners awaiting the return of their furious officer.

War department target tower Bethune, *1944.*

Straddling the target! 1945.

Despite the odd incident like this the men who crewed the target-towers loved the job, partly due to the danger which gave us a rush of adrenaline as we sped through the water with shells whistling through the sky nearby. Ironically the closest brush with death I was to have on the target-tower wasn't while we carrying out our towing duties but when we were safely out of the water in dry-dock. I was up on the conning tower giving the roof a lick of paint, approximately thirty-five feet above ground level (the conning tower being above the wheelhouse), when I lost my footing on wet paint and sailed out into space. The *Bethune* was housed in a purpose-built steel cradle and as I fell backwards I wondered what I was going to hit first, and was sure it wasn't going to be pleasant. Sure enough halfway to the ground I landed on my back on one of the diagonal iron support girders, luckily managed to keep my head from slamming into it and from there commenced a rapid slide, head-first down to the ground. When I came to a stop I didn't dare open my eyes, let alone move, for fear of what damage I might have done myself. Some of my crew-mates rushed over and carried me back on board the launch, stripped me down and checked me over for injuries. By the time I opened my eyes and began to try moving my arms and legs my crew-mates were amazed as they couldn't even find a single scratch, whereas they had been expecting the worst when they saw me fall.

All I could think of was to chalk another one up to my guardian angel who had been looking out for me for a number of years now and had brought me safely through the war, though my back ached for a couple of weeks after.

The crews of the War Department target-towers were a close-knit group of men, and we got on well with the army boys as well, though there was always a healthy amount of good-natured banter going on when we met them for a beer in the evening, usually centred on their obviously futile attempts to get anywhere close to our target, though in truth we were usually more than impressed with how accurately they could land a shell. Although I loved the work, I had other responsibilities by now; our first daughter June was born in September 1947, and a second, Linda, in October 1950.

In the spring of 1951 I suffered another accident, this time not my fault, when a boatman didn't notice me as I was kneeling down coiling up a mooring rope, and he somehow managed to find my left eye with the sharp end of his boathook. I spent several days with my eye swathed in a bandage, and wasn't sure that I hadn't lost my sight until the dressing was removed. Once again I was lucky, and tests showed that I had suffered no lasting damage. With this, and the fact that working on the south coast meant that I was stationed away from home most of the time, I could see that it wasn't fair on Hilda having to bring the girls up single-handed, even though she had the support of her mother and family who lived nearby in Charlton. By the autumn of 1951 I decided that I couldn't put off the decision any longer, so with a heavy heart handed in my notice and quit the target-towers. I left on the Friday and travelled back to London, Hilda being delighted that I was back home full-time. I didn't intend to stay unemployed for long, though, so determined that I would enjoy one weekend off and then set about securing work on the following Monday. I wasn't sure what I was going to do next, but I remembered a chat I had had with a man I met when we had taken one of the War Department boats up the Thames to central London. We had taken in tow a barge that had come adrift from its moorings and a Port of London Authority (PLA) inspector had arrived to take some details, a man called Tom MacPherson. He was interested in the big, powerful-looking, target-towing launch and we had fallen into conversation. He had watched me manoeuvre the launch in the narrow confines close to shore where the barge had drifted and told me then that he would be pleased to recommend me if ever I felt like giving the PLA a try, and it was this that I had in mind to try once I had quit the War Department.

Army Form C.330

THE WAR DEPARTMENT

Civilian Employee's Certificate of Service

THIS IS TO CERTIFY THAT ACCORDING TO OFFICIAL RECORDS

Mr. Thomas Thompson MATHIESON

HAS BEEN EMPLOYED IN THE WAR DEPARTMENT AS FOLLOWS :—

Period of Employment

From :— 15 July 1944 To :— 29 Sept 1951.

Grades in which Employed	Scales of Pay
T/Able Seaman.	127/2 x 1/- to 130/10.

Rate of Pay on Termination of Employment 130/10 per week.

Nature of Duties Seafaring

Reason for Termination of Employment Own request

Assessments of Ability, Conduct and Health

Ability Very good

Conduct Very good

Health Very good

Special Remarks

Establishment

Signature

Œ, 23 Coy., R.A.S.C. (Water Transport)
for the Permanent Under-Secretary
of State for War

23 COY. R.A.S.C.
26 SEP 1951
(WATER TRANSPORT)
PLYMOUTH

Date 26 Sep. 51

War Department Certificate of Service, 1951.

Come Monday morning I was on the bus bright and early to Woolwich where the PLA offices were based, and the policeman standing guard at the entrance to the docks furnished me with a pass. The harbourmaster, Captain Letts, agreed to see me in his office straight away and after studying my discharge papers and questioning me on previous experience asked me when I could start as a boatman. Not wanting to give him time to change his mind I replied: "I can start here and now if you want me to!", but he laughed, told me to go home, tell my wife the good news and assured me that the next morning would be fine. I didn't realise it at the time, but that next day when I turned up for work was the beginning of a career on the Thames that would span the next thirty years.

The Port of London Authority was responsible for nearly one hundred miles of the river Thames and employees were expected to have a good knowledge of the entire length, though I would be working on what was called the mid-section, that being the stretch from London Bridge down-river to Erith in Kent. To start with I worked twelve-hour shifts, and these would always start with an hour-long clean and scrub for the boat, inside and out and taking care to polish all the brass-work. We had two launches on our section of river, the *Ray* and the *Roding*, plus a launch that we used on day-shifts only, the *Ravensbourne*. after they had been made ship-shape we would commence our patrol. Our first task was to make a list of all the ships on the river for the Lloyds of London registry of shipping, as in those days London was still a thriving, bustling, commercial port and quite often we would have ships queuing down the river, waiting their turn to find room to dock and off-load their cargoes. The shipping list would need to be with Lloyds in London by one o'clock in the afternoon, so this was the start of our daily routine.

One of our primary tasks was to identify and mark the sites of boats and barges that had foundered and sunk in the river, whether due to bad weather, collision, or cause unknown. To begin with I was amazed at the frequency with which this happened, as it seemed we were marking a new wreck at least every day, but as I say the Thames was a much busier port then than it is now. If a craft had sunk close to shore we would normally have no trouble identifying its position and laying a hazard warning flag, but if it had gone down in the working channel then we would have to sweep for it using cables strung between our two boats, then ensure it was well marked by wreck buoys, flags and/or lights; this was particularly important if the salvage department wasn't able to come and lift the vessel straight away. At this time there were still very many unmarked ships that had been sunk in the river by enemy action and it was a good many years before all of these were identified and dealt with. Some of our jobs were not so pleasant, especially on those occasions when we discovered human corpses in the river, either floating on the surface or lying on the bottom in the shallows at low tide. Many of these were here as the result of accidents or suicide, but the bodies that were trussed up and weighted down were victims of feuds in the London underworld and we would stay at the site until the arrival of the river police.

After a couple of years of shift-work as ordinary boatman I applied for a transfer to day-work and was promoted to the position of coxswain on the motor launch *Nore*, which came to be known as the "Royal Barge" when she took part in the coronation celebrations of Queen Elizabeth in 1953. The *Nore* was a beautiful-looking river launch built with classical lines and lots of highly polished mahogany, with twin diesel engines capable of pushing her fourteen tons to a speed in excess of twenty knots and she was the jewel in the crown of the PLA fleet. The nature of the work I was doing changed from ad-hoc river patrolling duties to being aboard a boat doing more of an ambassadorial role for the PLA, the *Nore* being available to carry VIPs and dignitaries on trips along the river. On 12th June, 1953, we carried a young Queen Elizabeth and Prince Phillip upriver after a banquet at the Guildhall in the City of London, disembarking them at the Festival Pier. The Queen

ML Nore, *the 'Royal Barge'.*

Queen Elizabeth and Prince Phillip coming aboard the Nore, *12th June, 1953.*
Thomas holding the mooring rope at the stern.

would be back on board the *Nore* in 1977 for a river pageant celebrating her Silver Jubilee, while The Queen Mother, Prince Charles and Princess Margaret were all passengers at various times. I can recall world leaders such as French president De Gaulle, American president Truman, and Soviet leader Khruschev enjoying the sights of London from her decks. Our boss, Commander Parmiter, would always be present on these occasions, as would a PLA butler, someone you would be unlikely to find working on the river these days. We would carry business leaders and celebrities, some of whom were looking for locations along the river to shoot their movies, but I think the VIP passengers we most enjoyed having on board were the ex-naval men such as Prince Phillip and Lord Mountbatten. They would be at home on a ship or boat under any circumstances and were always very relaxed and happy to chat with the crew.

On one occasion in 1964 we were heading back to Tower Pier when I recognised Sir Winston Churchill waiting all alone at the end of the jetty. This was the first time I had seen him since the momentous VE Day, so as we were tying up I made up my mind to approach him and see if we could be of any assistance. To my disappointment a naval launch appeared and whisked him off to a battleship lying at anchor on the other side of the river before I had a chance to speak, and I never got another opportunity. Shortly after this near-encounter we received the news that Sir Winston had died, on 24th January, 1965, which was a great sadness to those of us who felt that no-one else could have led the country to victory as he did, and the whole country mourned the passing of one of Britain's most-loved leaders.

I was given the opportunity to pay my respects and honour the great man in a most unexpected way, as the *Nore* was chosen to lead the river procession bearing his body along the Thames, though the coffin itself would be onboard another PLA launch, *Havengore*. Churchill lay in state in the Palace of Westminster for three days before his funeral, and over 300,000 people filed past his coffin in that time. On the morning of 30th January his remains were transported by a gun carriage, pulled by a gun-crew of naval ratings, from Westminster to St. Paul's Cathedral. Our small flotilla had set out from Gravesend in Kent, keeping formation all the way up-river, until we arrived at Tower Pier at precisely 11 o'clock, the exact time Churchill's body arrived at St. Paul's for the commemoration service, for which I was commended. When the service was over he was carried, once more on the gun carriage, down to Tower Pier, as 90 guns were fired by the Tower of London battery, one for each year of his life.

We had a number of Winston's closest family and friends on board the Nore by the time his body was piped aboard the *Havengore*, and as we slowly swung out from the pier to mid-river, with 300 million people watching on television around the world, a nineteen-gun salute rang out. The short trip upriver was also marked by a fly-past of sixteen English Electric Lightning fighter jets, and in tribute the dockers of Hays Wharf lowered their cranes to the river as we passed. We were all feeling the emotion of the occasion by the time we reached Festival Pier and his coffin was disembarked to continue the journey by train from Waterloo to his final resting place at St. Martin's churchyard, Bladon, in Oxfordshire. For the first time in its history the Port of London struck medals for the employees who had the honour to participate in this historic occasion, and this is still one of my most prized possessions.

PORT OF LONDON AUTHORITY.
P.O. BOX No. 242.
TRINITY SQUARE.
LONDON, E.C.3.

IDLEY PERKINS
RECTOR-GENERAL

Telephone: ROYAL 2000

2nd November, 1965

Dear Mr. Mathieson,

Funeral of the late
Sir Winston Churchill

The Authority have decided that Sir Winston Churchill Commemorative Crowns should be presented to you and other members of the staff who were intimately concerned with the funeral arrangements of this great statesman.

I should like to take the opportunity of thanking you personally for the part you played on this solemn and historic occasion.

Yours sincerely,

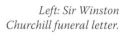

Left: Sir Winston Churchill funeral letter.

Above: Churchill funeral commemorative medal.

BORN A BEACHCOMBER

Chapter Nine

In 1955 Hilda and I moved, with our two girls, June and Linda, to 17 Eversley Road in Charlton, a three-bedroom terraced house in what was a typical working class area of London on the south side of the river. This was a close-knit community with a lot of the residents having working connections with the river and more particularly the docks, and was ideal for us as Hilda's family lived just round the corner. Cyril, her oldest brother, had succumbed to wounds received at El Alamein and died in 1947, while youngest brother Reg spent a lot of his time in Germany working for the War Office after surviving several years of jungle fighting against the Japanese in the Far East, with third brother Stan working as an accountant at a wine-importers in central London. From Eversley Road we could hear the crowd roar from "The Valley", the home of Charlton Athletic, and the whole family would often spend the afternoon at football if the "Addicks" were playing at home. The Valley was the biggest club ground in the country in those days and Charlton had often attracted huge crowds, the record being over 75,000, though the counting wasn't particularly accurate and combined with the number of kids who "bunked in" many thought the true figure was well over 100,000.

I now had what I considered my perfect job, where I would work happily for the next thirty years. The Thames is an ever-changing environment, no two days ever being the same, always affected by wind, weather and tides, as well as interactions with the huge population living along its banks and the effects of changing economic circumstances. One of the biggest surprises I ever had, and one that raised mixed emotions in me, happened the day I was motoring down to Greenwich Pier to pick up Commander Parmiter and noticed a ship tied up nearby. It had been part of my duties when I first started with the PLA to take note of all shipping present in

Hilda, myself, June, Hilda's mother Ada and Linda, London, 1958.

the river, so I still made a mental note of names and registrations when passing, and on this occasion the name meant more to me than usual – *Durmitor*. This ship had borne me to captivity in Somalia, though she was obviously being looked after a lot better than she had been back in the early war years, and now here she was looming over me in the heart of London. My thoughts travelled back over twenty years to that time on the Indian Ocean when my personal circumstances were very different; when food, water and a good night's sleep were scarce luxuries and neither my companions or I had any idea whether we would survive or not. I had certainly been one of the lucky ones, both as a captive at sea and later on land, but many people I had known had not shared my good fortune and never saw home again. Although a poignant reminder of those times, I held no grudge against the *Durmitor*, as she and her crew had been as much victims of the circumstances of the times as me, but it certainly made me more than a little reflective as we motored past her. Despite the lack of care and attention that had been shown to *Durmitor* during the war, and despite changing sides several times, she managed to survive and was still in working order. After being abandoned by Lt. Dehnel at Kismaayo, she had been seized by the British in 1943 and renamed the *Radwinter*. At the end of the war she was returned to her home port of Dubrovnik where she once more became *Durmitor*, resuming her cargo-carrying duties until she went to the breakers in 1963.

Although I was now settled in London my parents were always keen for us to spend time with them in Shetland, so most summers would be spent in Unst and also the occasional Christmas. Of my brothers, Alex had spent time at sea in the merchant service, but by the late 1940s was a lighthouse keeper in the north of Scotland. Jimmy Andrew and Johnny Charlie had their time at sea but returned to the croft after the war, while Willie Gibbie had served in the RAF but had also returned home. My eldest sister Anne had been in service with a wealthy Shetland family for a time but had also returned to Buddabrake, while my other surviving sister, Mima, had joined the ATS during the war and been stationed in the Midlands, where she had met her future husband. The ATS was the women's equivalent of the

Mima, mother, Antonia, Jimmy, father (plus Mima's children Dorothy and David), c.1955.

army, with over 200,000 enlisted by the end of the war, and they would be tasked with doing anything the men's army did except actually fight. In the late 1940s Mima's circumstances had changed to the extent that she now wanted to return home, so I sent her the money she needed to get herself and her two children, David and Dorothy, to Unst where they were welcomed back by the rest of the family.

In 1961 Hilda gave birth to our son, Stephen, and so by now when we arrived back home at Buddabrake for the summer holidays there was always a very full house. Our Shetland holidays were the highlight of our year, even though the journey from London was an arduous affair. We would order a cab to take us from our house in Charlton to Victoria coach station, and lots of the neighbours would be there to wave us off. The Aberdeen-bound

Hilda, Linda and Stephen, Buddabrake, 1963.

coach would depart at seven o'clock in the evening, and after a very early morning stop at Carlisle would arrive at approximately eight o'clock the following morning. We would then spend the day visiting with our cousins Anne-Barbara and her son George in Menzies Street, Torry, before catching the night boat that evening.

The ferry to Lerwick was normally a very sociable affair, with live music, dancing and drinking until the wee hours. We usually had a cabin, as the crossing would last twelve to fourteen hours, though sometimes these were all booked up so the family had to make do with seats, benches or the floor to sleep on. The ship, the *St. Clair* in those days, would dock at seven o'clock in the morning and we would then seek out the overland bus. This was something of a bone-shaker of a ride, not much suspension to speak of and very poor, single track roads heading north, nothing like the excellent quality of modern roads in the islands. The seats were rather uncomfortable, but not as bad as the fold-down seats in the aisles normally reserved for the kids. At Toft we would disembark, taking our luggage with us down a seaweed-covered slipway onto a small boat that would take us on the twenty-minute trip to Yell. Luggage would then be struggled with up the Ulsta slip to the waiting overland bus. This would then take us through Yell to the terminal at Gutcher, though on some occasions it would

Buddabrake, 1960s.

offload us at Mid-Yell where we would have to take a second bus on to the north. One more ferry-ride, one more struggle with the luggage onto the slipway at Belmont, and the last overland bus was waiting to transport us to Burrafirth. The sight of the house appearing at the top of the Buddabrake road was one that meant our long trek north was over and the sight of my brothers and sisters waiting for us in the porch made it all worthwhile, as well as the long, golden sands forming a backdrop to our old home.

All the men worked on the croft, though Johnny also had a job in the local sandstone quarry on Setters Hill. This was the only source of household income other than what the croft generated, but lack of money never affected the house's reputation as having one of the most welcoming kitchens to visit in Unst. Most crofters on the island in those days would ferment a most powerful Unst "hom bru", a sour mash that would sit unassumingly in a barrel in the corner of the kitchen until unleashed on unwary visitors. Most evenings would find at least one or two of the neighbours sat through for a yarn, and often this would be all the excuse my brothers needed to initiate a sociable evening, starting with a glass of brew followed up by the appearance of a fiddle and sometimes an accordion, and the party would get into full swing. The rugs on the floor would be flung into a corner and the music would begin, accompanied by the stomp of work-boots on lino, as bodies span around the improvised dance-floor with small children, cats and dogs adding to the melee whilst doing their best to avoid being trampled underfoot. These gatherings would occur on a regular basis, going on into the small hours of the morning with only an occasional halt being called when my sisters would lay meat and tatties on the table.

Burrafirth was a community full of Shetland characters in those days; apart from my brothers and sisters there was Bertie and Ena Mathieson from Lower Buddabrake, Peerie Willie Mathewson from Stoorigarth, Willie and Rena Henderson from Sotland, Peter Sinclair and Anderina from Seaview, Johnny Sutherland and Bella from Sandfield, Alec and Minnie Sinclair from Stackhoull, Patrick and Minnie Fordyce from Annsbrae. These were all from families who had crofted and fished in and around Burrafirth for generations, who knew the meaning of deprivation and hard work, but who also knew how to let their hair down when the opportunity arose. The only one who couldn't let his hair down was Willie Gibbie who had lost all his after his close encounter with the cliff-face as mentioned previously, but he would make up for this by being the life and soul of most gatherings. He was also a marvellous story-teller and carried on the age-old Shetland tradition of oral history telling, having memorised many tales told him by

Thomas behind Johnny Charlie (lef) and Willie Gibbie, Buddabrake, 1970.

"Peerie Alec's shop", Burrafirth. Alex Priest and Bill Sinclair (my old Burrafirth school pal) plus ginger tom mouser! (Courtesy of Brian Edwardson)

old Burrafirth folk now long since departed, this being the other favourite way for visitors to spend an entertaining evening at Buddabrake.

One of his stories concerned an old boy called Freddie Stickle, who was a friend of my grandfather Scollay. Freddie had very poor eyesight but would rarely wear his spectacles outside of the house, not wanting to lose or break them. Now, one day he was crossing the sand at Burrafirth, intending to make for Buddabrake via the steep cliff path below the house. As he neared the boats at the foot of the cliff he noticed a figure, apparently somebody sitting in deep contemplation on one of the Root Stacks, a line of rocks that jutted out into the firth and from where we sometimes launched the boat at low tide. The silent figure was, in fact, a large dog-otter who was standing on the rock drying himself and dozing in the sunshine, no doubt after a successful fishing expedition, but who Freddie now mistook for his friend, deep in thought.

"Ho, Scollay, what's all doing with ye?" Freddie shouted.

At this, of course, the startled otter dived off the rock and disappeared, leaving a dumbstruck Freddie to stare out over the water where he believed his friend had flung himself. Regaining a little composure Freddie then started up the path as fast as his legs would carry him, arriving breathless in the kitchen at Buddabrake and recounting the story to Scollay's puzzled family, ending his tale with "and man, Scollay disappeared into the great blue boil!"

Scollay's mother herself made Freddie sit down and insisted that he have a cup of tea to calm his nerves, though he thought a medicinal dram of whisky would suffice. The assembled family were slightly perturbed by Freddie's story, though most thought it a dubious tale, especially the older members who knew Freddie and his imagination well. Still, it was not unknown for strange things to happen around Burrafirth, including mysterious disappearances (which were usually blamed on the "peerie folk"), and it was not until an hour later, when Scollay himself appeared after being away from the house working on the croft, that the tale was fully discredited and a logical explanation found with the otter as the hero/culprit, much to the disappointment of the younger family members. Scollay laughed when he heard the story of his startling disappearance and how agitated Freddie had been in the recounting, clapping him on the back and advising that Freddie should either cut down on the Unst "bru" or start wearing his glasses more often.

Another story concerned Tommy Williamson, an old crofter who lived with his wife near Ungirsta, between Burrafirth and Haroldswick. One summer's day in the early 1900s the two of them were out ploughing when a strange buzzing noise was heard. They looked round about for the source of the noise, which was getting louder and louder, but could see nothing. The noise became alarming loud and finally Tommy looked up to the sky to see a strange machine approaching them on a course that would take it directly overhead. This was the first aeroplane that had ever been seen in Unst, but of course Tommy had absolutely no idea what it was he was looking at in the sky above. He turned to his wife and in a quiet, calm voice said:

"Well, it looks like it's the end of the world – we'd better stable the horses!"

Willie was a born storyteller and would mimic the voices of his subjects brilliantly, always keeping his audience engrossed and always raising a laugh, no matter how often they might have heard the same tale. Television only came to Unst in the 1970s and even then it was very much a hit and miss affair, usually a snowstorm for a picture and hissing and crackling for sound, so gathering everybody around the range in the dimly-lit kitchen to listen to local folk-tales was a far more entertaining way of passing the evening. The children would sit wide-eyed listening to tales of the "Faerie Knowe" near Tonga on the west coast, where fiddle music had

"Peerie" Willie Mathewson and Willie Gibbie Mathieson, 1924.

"Peerie" Willie Mathewson and Willie Gibbie Mathieson, 1974.
(Courtesy of Jonathan Wills)

been heard coming from inside the hill itself on many different occasions by folk who were heading back in the deepening twilight from tending their sheep or searching for driftwood along the nearby shore. Over the years the "Knowe" had even been associated with mysterious disappearances of men and women, and it was believed that the "peerie folk" who lived in the hill would try to take for their own any travellers who were abroad at night in the vicinity of their subterranean home. Or the story of Joseph Mathieson, who scaled the cliff of Hermaness in 1843 to catch the last sea eagle in Shetland on its 500 feet high eyrie, where he crossed its wings and killed it, returning with the body and presenting it to the laird at Buness, and for which he was rewarded with a sack of flour. The men would sit listening to the tales, interjecting with a comment or two of their own every now and again and ready with their own stories when the chance came, fortifying themselves with "bru", beer and a "corn" or two of whisky, while, as with the nights of song and dance, the women would busy themselves preparing food for their guests, often into the early hours of the morning.

If our summer evenings were not spent at the entertainment in the kitchen then we would be out fishing in our wonderful green and white painted Shetland Model boat *Doris*. Often with all the children aboard, both ours and Mima's, we four brothers would take the boat out to the best fishing spots in Burrafirth, sometimes at the very mouth of the voe itself, with two of us rowing and two preparing the lines with bait. Bait would normally be either fresh mackerel or "giddeks", sand eels dug up from the beach, and the lines would usually be heavy with piltocks, flounders, and cod, which would be put into the bottom of the boat before being bagged when we landed. There was little thought given to safety in those days, with nobody wearing as much as a life-vest let alone the boat carrying a radio; we were all very confident in our ability to handle a boat at sea, though occasionally the wind would get up and the swell rise enough to make Hilda uncomfortable. We would never be too far from shore, unlike in my grandfather's day, so some hard pulling on the oars would get us back to calmer waters within an hour or so. The boat was open, which, though it meant that it handled much better than a boat encumbered by a cabin, also meant that all inside were likely as not to get a good soaking on a trip out, either from salt spray or a sudden downpour. This never dampened the enthusiasm of the children or the adults aboard, though it made the return to Buddabrake and the warmth of the kitchen all the more appealing.

We only had one accident in all the years that we were out in the boat, and that was in 1961, when we allowed the two eldest girls, June and

Dorothy, to row the boat back to shore. Instead of heading her straight in they managed to put her side-on to the incoming waves, which resulted in a particularly large roller capsizing us and dumping us into the drink. Luckily we were close inshore at the time and well within our depth, especially as Hilda was holding Stephen, who was only a few months old at the time, and she managed to keep her footing and scramble quickly up the beach. We made sure the rest of the children were fine before we saw to the boat and looked to salvage as much of our equipment as we could, though we ended up losing most of the evening's catch. The children all thought that it was the best fun in the world, especially as they were all soaking wet, and we managed to right the *Doris* without too much hardship, so in the end there was no harm done, though my sisters took a different view when we arrived at the house in our sopping wet clothes.

Another holiday favourite was a trip out to the Flugga when it was being replenished with provisions or there was a change of keepers. The lighthouse relief boat, named the *Grace Darling* after the famous heroine, was crewed by my brothers and other close relations, with the skipper having his home in the boatman's cottage that formed part of the complex of buildings at "The Ness" where the lighthouse keepers' families also stayed. The core of the crew were my brothers Willie and Johnny, cousins Bertie Mathieson and "Peerie" Willie Matthewson, Peter Sinclair from Seaview and Tommy Bruce from Stove. The skipper from the war years to the seventies was Lowrie Edwardson, followed in 1974 for a couple of years by a young chap who had recently come to live in Unst, Jonathan Wills, and finally my cousin Ali Sinclair from Stackhoull, who was the boatman until the relief boat was deemed surplus to requirements (the Flugga was automated in 1995).

Going out in the *Grace Darling* was a real treat, firstly because we were out in a boat with an engine (and a good reliable diesel one at that) and didn't have to row, secondly because we often had a trip round beneath the gannet colonies on the Hermaness cliffs and the surrounding skerries, and thirdly because we would often land on the Flugga itself and walk up to have a chat and a bite to eat with the keepers. One who became a personal friend of mine was Alec Tulloch, who later retired and lived near us in Baltasound and with whom I passed many a happy day fishing in later years. The view from the lighthouse is, of course, stunning, and it is just such a shame that folk can no longer have a job and live in some of the most spectacular locations in the country, as all the lighthouses are now automated. Muckle Flugga also had a profound effect in a different way on my family in that my

Flugga boat crew on the slipway at the Ness. Lowrie's last day, Jonathan's first. From left: Willie Gibbie, unknown, Bertie Mathieson, Jonathan Wills, Peter Sinclair, "Peerie" Willie Mathewson, Lowrie Edwardson, 1974.
(Courtesy of Brian Edwardson)

Grace Darling *crew, 1980. Clockwise from front: "Peerie" Willie Mathewson, Johnny Charlie, Ali Sinclair (skipper), Bertie Mathieson, Tommy Bruce, Willie Gibbie.*
(Courtesy of Billy Fox)

Muckle Flugga lighthouse with Outstack far right. (Courtesy of Yolanda Bruce)

younger daughter, Linda, met one of the keepers, Lawrence Johnstone, on a trip there; a chance meeting that later resulted in their marriage and two more grandchildren for Hilda and I.

Landing at the Flugga was rarely straightforward, the thirty-five feet, heavily-laden boat needing to be manoeuvred between Muckle and Peerie Flugga, avoiding the jagged rocks lying in wait should she stray slightly off-course, and then brought to lie alongside the concrete jetty with just the right choice of wave, where the keepers would fling ropes out to the crew which then had to be made fast in double-quick time before the next wave either took the boat back out or crashed her against the unforgiving structure. If the weather and waves were suitable we would take a turn around the Outstack on the way back (Britain's most northerly point), and at different times of the year would sometimes see sperm and minke whales, basking sharks, dolphins and porpoises around the boat, while in the skies we would watch bonxies attempt to take puffins or kittiwakes out of the air, and huge flocks of gannets would dive into the sea at breakneck speed, resembling guided missiles, homing in on the shoals beneath. Quite often the enterprise of these incredible creatures would go unrewarded, though, as the bonxies would note those that had made successful dives and then harass them unmercifully until they spewed up their catch, which the bonxies would then seize upon in the water.

Our holidays in Unst continued until I retired in 1980; the three children had all left home by then, and Hilda and I decided that we had lived in London long enough, and now was the time to return to my home island. My sister Antonia had died in 1977 and my elder brother Jimmy in 1978, so I was keen to spend more time with my remaining siblings and other family. Much as I would have loved to move back to Burrafirth, it was just not feasible or practical at the time, so we moved to a brand new house in Nikkavord Lea, Baltasound, which was still close enough to Buddabrake to be within easy reach by car. Unfortunately neither Hilda nor I had ever taken time to learn to drive, but Hilda decided to take up this new challenge at the age of sixty-three, and though she never ended up passing her driving test she was still proficient enough to drive on Unst, where a provisional licence was all that was needed at that time. The only thing I was ever happy steering was a boat, so I purchased a twenty-foot clinker built boat, the *Good Hope*, adding a cuddy cabin the following year. I had many years happy fishing out of her, and quite a few adventures, as I never did seem able to find a reliable engine! One of my fishing buddies was the old laird, Mr Edmondston, who was always up for a trip off even though he was considerably older than me. On one occasion we had the lines out on the far side of Balta Isle, when a bank of fog came in and showed no signs of clearing, so we decided to haul anchor and head for home. Unfortunately the main engine decided it was not going to play ball and refused to start, at which point we discovered that the spare motor had been lying in salt water for some time and was also dead to the world. The only thing for it was to row, which was not the easiest option on the *Good Hope* due to the cabin I had built for'ard making her a little less aerodynamic, but we managed to make a safe landing back at Baltasound pier after several hours of exertion. We had made the right choice as the fog had become denser as we rowed and a large swell was coming in from the east, but not a bad effort as I was in my mid-seventies at this time and the laird was in his nineties.

The 1980s were momentous years for Shetland, with many changes that had been presaged by the earlier discovery of North Sea oil and the development of the industry in the 1970s that made Shetland its focal point. In those years it was not obvious what the scale of the changes would be, and there were still enough folk carrying on with traditional ways of crofting, crafting and fishing to keep the light burning for the ways of life that had kept these islands going for the last thousand years. By the end of the 80s more of the old names and faces had disappeared, and the old ways and the traditional communities were now in terminal decline. New industry, new jobs, new wealth had arrived, and with them all the benefits for improving the infrastructure of the islands beyond all recognition.

Thomas and Hilda, 2010.

This new prosperity has brought with it new and greater aspirations for the population, which the old ways cannot possibly compete with. In 1985 my brother Johnny passed away, followed by my last surviving brother, Willie, the great story-teller, in 1989. Mima left Buddabrake to stay with

Stephen and youngest grandchild, Cormac, on Burrafirth beach, 2013.

Thomas at his favourite fishing spot on Burrafirth beach.

her daughter and now the old house was empty and quiet for the first time in many, many years. Mima herself died the following year.

Here, in the second decade of the twenty-first century, I am the last of the "Buddabrake Boys", my brothers and sisters having all passed away many years ago. Hilda and I are now living in retirement in Lerwick, though my thoughts will always stray to that house nestled into the side of the firth and to that northern beach, still looking out for whatever the tides may bring.